THE TWO OF ME

2 Corinthians 5:17 KJV
Therefore if any man [be] in Christ, [he is] a
new creature: old things are passed away;
behold, all things are become new.

The Two of Me

Stephanie M. White

To order additional copies of this book, or HEAVEN ON EARTH or FAITH IS WORTH FIGHTING FOR, contact:

HTTPS://WHITESTEPHANIE83.WIXSITE.COM/

HEAVENONEARTHFORYOU

Contents

Two Natures, One Person 7

The Source of the New Nature....................... 15

One Plus One Equals Zero............................ 28

It's Not About Me.. 40

Who's Serving Who? 52

Two Kinds of Love 62

Getting to Know YOU 72

Spiritual Growth.. 84

Mature Matters 92

My Two Minds 101

Live Like.. 111

Mr. Do Right...119

Confident Christian 127

Victory Over the Flesh 133

The Conclusion..143

CHAPTER 1

TWO NATURES, ONE PERSON

John 3:3-6 KJV

Jesus answered and said unto him, "Verily, verily, I say unto thee, except a man be born again, he cannot see the kingdom of God." Nicodemus saith unto Him, "How can a man be born when he is old? Can he enter the second time into his mother's womb, and be born?" Jesus answered, "Verily, verily, I say unto thee, except a man be born of water and [of] the Spirit, he cannot enter into the kingdom of God. THAT WHICH IS BORN OF THE FLESH IS FLESH; AND THAT WHICH IS BORN OF THE SPIRIT IS SPIRIT."

That which is born of flesh is flesh and that which is born of Spirit is Spirit. What was Jesus articulating? Why did Jesus say we have to be "born again?" Being born again is a fundamental precept that we must understand as Christians. Jesus tells us that we must be born again because the first time we were born it was simply a birth of the flesh; it was not Spiritual. If we desire to see the kingdom of God we must be born *again* – something *Spiritual* must take place.

That which is born of the flesh is flesh and that which is born of the Spirit is Spirit; there are *two* natures in every born-again believer – two natures that must be recognized and understood. Once you receive Christ as your personal Lord and Savior the Bible then refers to you as being "born again." Something new has taken place; something new is given life inside of you.

John 10:10 KJV The thief cometh not, but for to steal, and to kill, and to destroy: I am come that they might have life, and that they might have [it] more abundantly.

Jesus Christ came to give us life; He came to give us this new nature. "Life" is defined as Spiritual life or life as God has it; this kind of life includes participating in the Divine nature. Jesus Christ comes to live inside of us when we receive Him and now we have the life of God at work within us. No longer are we simply carnal; we now have Spiritual life, as well. We now have the ability to take part in the Divine nature and leave our flesh behind.

Romans 8:2 AMP For the law of the Spirit of life [which is] in Christ Jesus [the law of our new being] has freed me from the law of sin and of death.

When we are participating in our Spiritual nature we are free from the law of sin and death. We cannot walk in the Spiritual nature and our flesh at the same time. We no longer have to live according to our flesh because Jesus died and gave us a new nature – a nature that is controlled by the Holy Spirit.

This Spiritual life has always been God's plan for us. Adam was given this life but Satan came to steal, kill, and destroy.

Romans 5:12 NIV Therefore, just as sin entered the world through one man, and death through sin, and in this way death came to all men, because all sinned.

After the fall of man, death (or life outside of the Spirit, i.e. the flesh) came to all men. The flesh would now reign in man. We would come into this world as sinners; and because of this, we would now need a Savior. Apart from Christ we have death – a life lived in the flesh followed by an eternity in hell; both of which are separation from God. Sin caused separation from God and we would now need to be connected to God. We would need to have life imparted to us; Jesus Christ came to do just that. He came to give us new life in the Spirit.

> 2 Corinthians 5:17 KJV Therefore if any man [be] in Christ, [he is] a new creature: old things are passed away; behold, all things are become new.

When discussing the new nature we find that it is also identified in Scripture as being "in Christ." When we read these two words we must understand that they are depicting our Spiritual nature. Who we are in Christ is who we are Spiritually. We find our new life, our Spiritual life, *in Christ*.

We have this new life but this does not mean that our old life is no longer present. We read that the old things are "passed away" and this can lead us to believe that the old nature is dead, but it is not; our flesh did not become lifeless and void of any power because we received Christ. The phrase "passed away" comes from a word that means "to come near or alongside." This new Spiritual nature you received came near or alongside the old nature of the flesh. We now have *two* natures and we must be aware of this. If we fail to realize that there are two parts to each one of us we will struggle through our lives as Christians.

The old nature, or the flesh, is our identity apart from Christ; it is who we are outside of Christ. This nature has no desire to be Spiritual. This nature *hates* the things of God. This nature participates *only* in sin; it is *impossible* for this nature to do *anything* Spiritual. **When we sin we must**

understand that we are operating in our carnal nature. We do not sin because we do not love God or because we are what some call "bad" Christians; we sin because we are in the flesh. It is just that simple. We do not have to wonder why we fall into the same sin over and over. We do not have to wonder why we do the things that we hate doing. When we understand what our flesh is and what it accomplishes we can avoid futile speculation. We can simply know that our flesh produces flesh.

> Romans 7:18 NIV I know that nothing good lives in me, that is, in my sinful nature. For I have the desire to do what is good, but I cannot carry it out.

> Romans 3:10-13 NIV As it is written: "There is no one righteous, not even one; there is no one who understands, no one who seeks God. All have turned away, they have together become worthless; there is no one who does good, not even one."

Nothing good, nothing Spiritual, dwells in the flesh. We are void of God in our flesh. In understanding this, we might ask, "Why did God leave us with the flesh?"

> Romans 8:20-21 NIV For the creation was subjected to frustration, not by its own choice, but by the will of the One who subjected it, in hope that the creation itself will be liberated from its bondage to decay and brought into the glorious freedom of the children of God.

The seventh and eighth chapters of Romans tell us that the flesh is a frustration (no kidding!). They also tell us that our Creator left us with this frustration on purpose and it then goes on to tell us why. He left us with our flesh in hope that we would find true freedom as a child of God. **The purpose our flesh serves is to lead us to Christ!** The flesh should make us feel so helpless that we run to Christ for the Spiritual help we require, but too many people assume that they can handle it on their own, in their flesh. When our flesh is not leading us to the Spirit it is not doing the work God designed it to do.

Our new nature, the Spirit, is our identity in Christ. It is who we are because of our union with Jesus. This nature cannot sin; it is *impossible* for the Spiritual nature to produce anything other than Spiritual fruit. If we are producing any Spiritual fruit we must appreciate what is taking place; we are producing Spiritual fruit because we are walking in the Spirit. We cannot produce Spiritual fruit outside of Christ. **We do not produce Spiritual fruit because we are "great" Christians or because we love God enough; we produce Spiritual fruit because we know that we require the Word and we abide in it. We fill ourselves with the Word of God and the Word produces Spiritual fruit in our lives. Spirit gives birth to Spirit.**

The Bible states that "all things *become* new;" the new nature *comes into being* or is *brought out* in us when we focus on who we are in Christ. Our union with Christ makes us Spiritual beings. This new nature will not take center-stage in your life as long as you are spotlighting the old nature. We have to let go of the old life if we want to take possession of the new life. We must begin to see ourselves according to who we are in Christ.

> 1 John 3:2-9 NIV Dear friends, now we are children of God, and what we will be has not yet been made known. But we know that when He appears, we shall be like Him, for we shall see Him as He is. Everyone

who has this hope in Him purifies himself, just as He is pure. Everyone who sins breaks the law; in fact, sin is lawlessness. But you know that He appeared so that He might take away our sins. And in Him is no sin. No one who lives in Him keeps on sinning. No one who continues to sin has either seen Him or known Him. Dear children, do not let anyone lead you astray. He who does what is right is righteous, just as He is righteous. He who does what is sinful is of the devil, because the devil has been sinning from the beginning. The reason the Son of God appeared was to destroy the devil's work. No one who is born of God will continue to sin, because God's Seed remains in him; he cannot go on sinning, because he has been born of God.

We are *now* children of God. When we receive Christ He provides us with this new identity not because of anything *we* have done but because of what *He* has done. We are *now* His offspring; we are now "of Him." The more we get to know who Christ is, the more we will understand our new identity. We need to see Christ for who He truly is. For example; we need to see Him as our righteousness if we are ever going to walk in righteousness and produce righteous fruit. If we look to ourselves for righteousness we will be disappointed; we will either fall into the pretense of pride or we will live in self-degradation. On our own we cannot attain what we need, but if we are looking to Christ we will find that we are abundantly supplied.

We must understand that these verses in the first book of John are dealing with our *two natures*. If we think these verses are referring to two different *people* we will become confused. We must realize that these verses are referring to one person who has two natures. **Understanding that you**

have two natures at work inside of you will keep you from misunderstanding the Word. The phrase, "No one who lives in Him keeps on sinning," can lead us to believe that if we sin we are not saved – *if* we do not divide between the flesh and the Spirit. No one who "lives in Him" will sin because LIVING IN HIM IS PARTICIPATING IN THE SPIRITUAL NATURE. When we do what is right (or more correctly, Spiritual) it is because we are walking in the Spiritual nature. **Avoiding sin can *only* be accomplished by our Spiritual nature. Only the Spirit can produce Spiritual fruit.** If we are doing what is sinful it is because we are operating in the flesh – the nature that is "of the devil." Jesus Christ came to destroy the works of the devil; He came to give us Spiritual life.

When we recognize ourselves according to our Spiritual nature we will understand that we *are* pure because *He* is pure. We will understand that we *are* righteous because *He* is righteous, and so on. Seeing ourselves this way will have nothing to do with arrogance; you see yourself this way when you realize your identity is found in Christ. Seeing yourself as pure, righteous, holy, and so on, will not produce pride; it will generate an abundance of thanksgiving.

> Psalms 7:17 NIV I will give thanks to the LORD because of His righteousness and will sing praise to the name of the LORD Most High.

When we recognize that our righteousness is found solely in Christ we will be overwhelmed with the feeling of thankfulness.

> 1 Corinthians 1:29-31 MSG That makes it quite clear that none of you can get by with blowing your own horn before God. Everything that we have--right

thinking and right living, a clean slate and a fresh start--comes from God by way of Jesus Christ. That's why we have the saying, "If you're going to blow a horn, blow a trumpet for God."

We will not take pride in what we do; we will take pride in what *God* has done when we understand that He is our Spiritual source. We will give Him the thanks and the praise for every Spiritual fruit produced in our lives. This is true humility. This is walking in your new identity.

The Word informs us that we have two identities and each has a purpose. The flesh should lead you to depend more on Christ and less on yourself. If your flesh is not leading you to Christ then it is not doing what it was created to do – it is being perverted. The Spirit's purpose is to reproduce Christ in the believer.

Both natures must be recognized for what they are and what they do. Let's continue on studying each.

CHAPTER 2

THE SOURCE OF THE NEW NATURE

Deuteronomy 32:46-47 NIV
He said to them, "Take to heart all the words I have
solemnly declared to you this day, so that you may
command your children to obey carefully all the
words of this law. They are not just idle words for
you--they are your life.   By them you will live long in the
land you are crossing the Jordan to possess."

John 6:63 NIV
The Spirit gives life; the flesh counts for nothing.
The words I have spoken to you
are Spirit and they are life.

The source of our Spiritual nature is Jesus Christ and He is
the Word (John 1:1). **If we are going to participate in our
Spiritual nature we are going to have to fill ourselves with
the Word of God.**

The Word of God is our life; it is our *Spiritual* life.
We must understand that the Word of God is our Spiritual
fuel. It is what will transport us from the flesh to the Spirit.
It will lead us to that promised land – that land of the Spirit –
and it will keep us in this Spiritual place. We need to take
the Word to heart; we need to "obey" the Word. The word
translated as "obey" in this verse in Deuteronomy is the
Hebrew word "shamar." This word means "to keep your
eyes on and to focus on." It also means "to hedge in as with

thorns." If we are going to enter into the Spiritual life that God has for us, then we are going to have to remain focused on the Word of God. We are going to have to hedge the Word in our lives; we are going to have to protect the Word and its preeminence in our lives. We must understand the value of the Word; we must understand that we can only take part in the Spiritual nature through the Word.

God never intended for us to endeavor to be Spiritual on our own. God is well aware of who we are and what we can do; after all, He is our Creator. He understands our limitations and that is why He has mercy on us (Psalms 103:13-14); *we* need to be aware of this (Romans 7:18). He knows that all of *our* righteousness is as filthy rags (Isaiah 64:6). Seeing this, we can know that He would not order us to "perform" all of His commandments in order for us to be blessed by Him or for Him to be pleased with us. If you knew that your child could not read, then you would never tell him or her that they had to read several chapters of a book before you would feed them. God is a loving Father. He knows that apart from Christ we can do nothing. He is not asking us to achieve; He is asking us to depend on Him.

Exodus 19:5-8 NIV Now if you *obey* Me fully and *keep* My covenant, then out of all nations you will be My treasured possession. Although the whole earth is Mine, you will be for Me a kingdom of priests and a holy nation.' These are the words you are to speak to the Israelites." So Moses went back and summoned the elders of the people and set before them all the words the LORD had commanded him to speak. The people all responded together, "We will do everything the LORD has said." So Moses brought their answer back to the LORD.

God told man to do something that was translated as "obey" and "keep."

OBEY: the Hebrew word "shama." Meaning to
hear intelligently, consent, consider, be content, declare, diligently, discern, give ear, (cause to, let, make to) hear (-ken, tell), indeed, listen, perceive, (make a) proclaim (-ation), publish, regard, report, shew (forth), surely, tell, understand, whosoever [heareth], witness.

KEEP: the Hebrew word "shamar." Meaning to
hedge about (as with thorns), that is, *guard*; generally to *protect, attend to*, etc.: - beware, be circumspect, take heed (to self), keep (-er, self), mark, look narrowly, observe, preserve, regard, reserve, save (self), sure, (that lay) wait (for), watch (-man).

What is translated many times as "obey" actually means to "hear intelligently," to be able to "understand" to the point that you can tell others. You can proclaim the Word because you have heard, considered, and regarded the Word. This kind of hearing is what *enables* us to do! We will show forth the Word when we are absorbing the Word. We can only obey, as the English language defines the word "obey," because we are abiding in the Word. The Word is the Seed to all Spiritual fruit.

To obey, the Hebrew word shama, also means to "be content." It is to be satisfied with the Word and nothing more. The Word is the *one* thing (Psalms 27:4, Luke 10:42) that we require. God wants us to realize that we are desperate for the Word; He wants us to recognize the Word as our *only* Spiritual Seed. When we are content with the Word we do not look to any other source. For example, we will not need God's promise for health *and* a good report from our doctor; we will only require the Word.

If you look at the Hebrew word for what has been translated as "keep" (and sometimes "obey") we see that it means to be diligent with the Word of God. What man has translated as keep actually means to guard or protect, to remain focused on, and to consider the Word something worth guarding in your life. We know that we only guard what is valuable; therefore, we must know the value of the Word if we are going to guard it in our lives. The Word will only be hedged in our lives when we understand its importance – we will not allow anything to touch the Word in our lives because we know how desperate we are for it.

Man twisted what God instructed them to do when He said to "shama" and "shamar" and decided they would "asah" instead.

> DO /ASAH: to *do* or *make*, accomplish, advance, become, bear, bestow (give, present), bring forth, bruise, be busy, (put in) execute (-ion), exercise, [fight-] ing man, finish, follow, fulfill, furnish, get, go about, govern, keep, labor, maintain, observe, be occupied, offer, bring (come) to pass, perform, practice, procure, provide, sacrifice, serve, show, vex, work (-man).

This word "asah" means to perform or accomplish something yourself. It is *man's* way of sacrificing – offering God *his* works. Man wanted to *accomplish* what the Word said, not be empowered by the Word. Man chose works over grace; he chose death over life. God gave man life when He gave him the Word, but man received the Word as a challenge or something to be attained.

> Romans 7:10 AMP   And the very legal ordinance which was designed and intended to bring life actually proved [to mean] death.

God gave the Word and the Word is life. Man turned that Word into death by treating it as nothing more than rules and regulations. Acts, verse thirty-eight of chapter seven, speaks of the Word as living oracles; Moses did not receive rules – he received the Words of life!

> Hosea 8:12 KJV   I have written to him the great things of My law, [but] they were counted as a strange thing.

Man took those words of life and perverted them and this perversion led to death –the flesh (Isaiah 28:9-13). Man counted or regarded the Word of God as a "strange thing." The Hebrew word translated as "strange thing" means to turn aside, to be a foreigner, to profane, and to commit adultery. When we turn aside from the Word of God we become a stranger in regards to the Word. We are not taking the Word in; instead, we are disrespectful and we are looking to other methods of producing fruit. We are betraying the Word when we ignore it and try to produce fruit without it.

When we turn the Word into mere rules and regulations, we are walking in the flesh and we can only accomplish works of the flesh.

> Romans 9:31-32 KJV   But Israel, which followed after the law of righteousness, hath not attained to the law of righteousness. Wherefore? Because [they

sought it] not by faith, but as it were by the works of
the law. For they stumbled at that Stumblingstone…

Man wanted to execute the law instead of trusting in
the Messiah to fulfill the law for him. Man decided it would
be better to trust in his own work. Man has the "I do it"
syndrome! Just like a little child, we emphatically declare, "I
do it!" We like to feel capable even though God tells us that
we are truly helpless on our own.

As we look at the definition for the Hebrew word
"asah" we see that it also means to "be busy" and "be
occupied." This reminds me of Martha (Luke 10:38-42), she
was busy with many things – she was occupied but she was
not doing anything of *Spiritual* value. Martha was so busy
but Mary sat at Jesus' feet and listened to every word He
spoke. Mary chose what would last (what was Spiritual or
what was eternal) and that was taking in the words that Christ
was speaking. Mary chose to "shama" and "shamar." We
need to ask ourselves if we are busy and occupied or are we
truly taking in the words of Christ and producing fruit that
will last. Are we, like Martha, choosing to "asah?"

Many of us want to offer God our works; we like to
feel as if what we do is a sacrifice to God. We like to believe
we are serving *Him*.

Acts 17:25 NIV And He is not served by human
hands, as if He needed anything, because He Himself
gives all men life and breath and everything else.

We must understand that *we* cannot serve God. *We*
have nothing to offer Him. Apart from Christ we are
Spiritually worthless. **We need to stop trying to offer God
something and we need to start receiving what He has to
offer us.**

What God wants to *enable* man to do, man wants to try to accomplish on his own.

> Romans 10:1-4 KJV Brethren, my heart's desire and prayer to God for Israel is, that they might be saved. For I bear them record that they have a zeal of God, but not according to knowledge. For they being ignorant of God's righteousness, and going about to establish their own righteousness, have not submitted themselves unto the righteousness of God. For Christ [is] the end of the law for righteousness to everyone that believeth.

God tells us that they were being ignorant of His righteousness; this word means "ignored." They ignored God's righteousness and set out to establish their own.

Christ is the end of the law or the end of works *when* we live by faith. They did not receive what Christ did for them; they did not live by faith. They wanted to do for themselves.

> Hebrews 8:9 KJV Not according to the covenant that I made with their fathers in the day when I took them by the hand to lead them out of the land of Egypt; because they continued not in My covenant, and I regarded them not, saith the Lord.

We need to do things God's way – not our way. God offered them the covenant of the Word but they did not want to "continue" in that covenant. Man wanted another covenant; man chose death instead of life.

> Isaiah 28:15 AMP Because you have said, We have made a covenant with death, and with Sheol (the

place of the dead) we have an agreement…in falsehood we have taken shelter.

Man's decision to live by works was a covenant of death. God has never required man to accomplish or perform Spiritual actions; this belief is falsehood. His covenant was always one of faith; it was always a life lived by every word that came from the mouth of God.

> Romans 1:28 NIV Furthermore, since they did not think it worthwhile to retain the knowledge of God, He gave them over to a depraved mind, to do what ought not to be done.

It did not appeal to them to have to abide in the Word. They did not want to have to take the Word in and keep their focus on it. They did not like God's plan; they did not want to continue in the Word. They wanted to come up with their own method and God let them do just that.

> Deuteronomy 5:28 KJV And the LORD heard the voice of your words, when ye spake unto me; and the LORD said unto me, I have heard the voice of the words of this people, which they have spoken unto thee: they have well said all that they have spoken.

God listened to man's plan of performance and he spoke in regards to their plan. When we look at the original text we find that God's reply basically means, "These people are clear about what they want and that is fine." God let man choose: choose life or choose death; either way, man had the freedom to choose.

In choosing to ignore the Word, we are planting the flesh and the flesh will only produce flesh, or in other words, death. Depending on our own strength and ability will never lead to anything Spiritual.

> Hosea 10:13-14 NIV   But you have planted wickedness, you have reaped evil, you have eaten the fruit of deception. Because you have depended on your own strength and on your many warriors, the roar of battle will rise against your people, so that all your fortresses will be devastated...

He allowed them to live in their flesh. He allowed them to sow seeds of the flesh and produce the fruit of the flesh. Living in their flesh led to works that "ought not to be done" – works that do not profit, works that will be destroyed.

> Hosea 5:7a NIV   They are unfaithful to the LORD; they give birth to illegitimate children.

Illegitimate children, or the fruits of the flesh, are produced when we are "unfaithful to the Lord." What does it mean to be unfaithful to the Lord?   The word that unfaithful is translated from is the Hebrew word "bagad." This word means to cover something up, to act covertly, and deal deceitfully.   We are covering up who Christ really is when we are trying to produce Spiritual fruit on our own. When we look at the Word as a rule book we are dealing deceitfully – the truth is that the Word is our life; the Word is what enables us to walk in the Spirit. Deciding to ignore the Word, and instead trying to live up to it, is deceitful living. We can only produce Spiritual fruit through Christ; we cannot live in the truth and attempt to be fruitful without Christ.

Hosea 14:8 NIV …your fruitfulness comes from Me.

The only Spiritual fruit we will produce is completed through Christ. We will only produce carnal fruit when we are not focused on Christ. What kind of fruit do you produce?

God has given us His perfect plan, but bear in mind that He has also given us a choice. God will not force us to do things His way; He gave us free will.

Acts 14:16 AMP In generations past He permitted all the nations to walk in their own ways.

God has not changed His mind; He was not one way in the Old Testament and a different way in the New Testament. His plan has always been the same – "shama" and "shamar." This plan is for man to live by every word that comes from the mouth of the Lord. The Word of God is taken in by reading the Word, speaking the Word, meditating on the Word, and so on. As we fill ourselves with the Word of God it will begin to come back out of us in the form of Spiritual fruit. Unfortunately, man has his own ideas – and God allows man to follow them.

The Israelites did not want to "shama" and "shamar" – they did not want what God was offering. They wanted to "asah" – they wanted to perform themselves. They instead wanted to offer God something.

Revelation 3:1-2 AMP And to the angel (messenger) of the assembly (church) in Sardis write: These are the words of Him Who has the seven Spirits of God [the sevenfold Holy Spirit] and the seven stars: I know your record and what you are doing; you are supposed to be alive, but [in reality] you are dead.

Rouse yourselves and keep awake, and strengthen and invigorate what remains and is on the point of dying; for I have not found a thing that you have done [any work of yours] meeting the requirements of My God or perfect in His sight.

Jesus said He knew what they were doing or accomplishing, but the problem was that they were doing it in their flesh. It may have *appeared* Spiritual, but it was *not* Spiritual. They were supposed to be alive – living in the Spirit, but they were dead – living in the flesh, and everything they were producing was dead. No action that we perform on our own will ever meet God's requirements; He requires that we live by faith.

Isaiah 66:2-3 AMP For all these things My hand has made, and so all these things have come into being [by and for Me], says the Lord. But this is the man to whom I will look and have regard: he who is humble and of a broken or wounded spirit, and who trembles at My word and reveres My commands. [The acts of the hypocrite's worship are as abominable to God as if they were offered to idols.] He who kills an ox [then] will be as guilty as if he slew and sacrificed a man; he who sacrifices a lamb or a kid, as if he broke a dog's neck and sacrificed him; he who offers a cereal offering, as if he offered swine's blood; he who burns incense [to God], as if he blessed an idol. [Such people] have chosen their own ways, and they delight in their abominations…

God is not looking for us to impress Him – He longs for us to understand that we *cannot* impress Him. All of the works we can muster up mean nothing to Him – they disgust

Him. He refers to them as lukewarm in Revelation and He declares that they are repulsive to Him. Lukewarm actions are the actions that appear Spiritual but are actually works of the flesh.

We can be doing something that God has said to do, but if we are doing it in our flesh it means nothing; it does not meet God's requirements. God requires faith, but man has a choice to make; we can choose our own ways. The Word of God unflinchingly declares that anything that is not of faith is sin (Romans 14:23). Faith can only come from following God's plan – "shama" and "shamar;" yet, man still wants to live outside of the Word.

> Romans 10:17 NIV Consequently, faith comes from hearing the message, and the message is heard through the Word of Christ.

We must wake up and understand the two natures. God instructs us to live by faith. This means to live in the Word since faith comes from hearing the Word. If we are going to live by faith we are going to have to abide in the Word of God. As we continue to abide in the Word faith is produced. Spiritual faith will then produce Spiritual actions. We cannot walk in the Spirit and fulfill the lusts of the flesh simultaneously, and we cannot walk in the flesh and produce Spiritual fruit. If we are walking in the Spirit we *will* produce Spiritual fruit and vice-versa.

> Hebrews 8:13 KJV In that He saith, A new [covenant], He hath made the first old. Now that which decayeth and waxeth old [is] ready to vanish away.

> Hebrews 9:8 NIV The Holy Spirit was showing by this that the way into the Most Holy Place had not yet

been disclosed as long as the first tabernacle was still standing.

You cannot try to work and sacrifice (asah) and live by grace (shama and shamar) at the same time. You have to lose the old life of performance to gain the new life of grace. If we are going to walk in this new nature we must abide in the Word of God and leave our works behind.

Man wanted to do, not hear or guard, the Word. Man wanted to perform, not have God work through them. Do you feel the same way? Are you trying to offer God something or are you receiving what He has to offer? God has supplied us with the Word of God; the Word is the Source of the new nature. What are you doing with it?

CHAPTER 3

ONE PLUS ONE EQUALS ZERO

Revelation 3:15-16 KJV
I know thy works, that thou art neither cold nor hot: I
would thou wert cold or hot. So then because thou art
lukewarm, and neither cold nor hot, I will spue thee out of
My mouth.

Lukewarm – let us take a deeper look at what this means. The Word of God tells us that lukewarm is neither hot nor cold; neither means "not too." These people were not too hot nor were they too cold – they were a mixture of both. There was not an abundance in either area. They were trying to live a Spiritual life in their flesh and they were only producing works of the flesh.

> 2 Timothy 3:5 KJV Having a form of godliness, but denying the power thereof: from such turn away.

A form is an appearance. We can *appear* to be godly – our works can *look* good, but if they are of the flesh they are worthless.

The people to which Second Timothy is referring are not simply in the flesh where we can *see* the "obvious" fruit of the flesh – they are *pretending* to be Spiritual; this makes God sick. Their actions appear Spiritual but they are not– they have no power.

The word "power" can be defined as miraculous power and ability. It also means strength and authority. The Spiritual actions that we accomplish through Christ have power; they have miraculous power. We see several Biblical characters demonstrating this power throughout God's Word. When we are abiding in the Word we have miraculous power and ability dwelling inside of us and we see it being worked out through us.

Some people only *appear* to be godly; they deny this miraculous power. To deny means to contradict or to reject; it means to give up. When we reject the Word of God we cannot operate in this miraculous power. By deciding to ignore the Word, we also decide to walk in the futility and weakness of the flesh. Walking in the flesh, whether it appears godly or not, can *only* produce works of the flesh.

> Galatians 6:8 KJV For he that soweth to his flesh shall of the flesh reap corruption; but he that soweth to the Spirit shall of the Spirit reap life everlasting.

We can rest assured that sowing to the flesh will produce a harvest of the flesh. We need to know what we are sowing. We need to understand the difference between the Spirit and the flesh. The Spirit will produce the fruit of the Spirit – life. Anything that is produced through Christ is eternal; it is not temporary. Any fruit that we produce on our own is fleeting.

> Matthew 6:5 NIV "And when you pray, do not be like the hypocrites, for they love to pray standing in the synagogues and on the street corners to be seen by men. I tell you the truth, they have received their reward in full."

The hypocrite performs in such a way that the fruit *appears* Spiritual; but be assured, there is no Spiritual root. This fruit is honored by man and seen by man, but this fruit means nothing to God. Appearance has its own reward and it is a temporary reward. The reward of the hypocrite begins and ends with man.

Having a *form* of godliness is denying the power. These works of mixture reject the miraculous power of God – they try to create their own strength and ability. They give up on the Word and turn to themselves to accomplish what only God can do in them and they are only producing counterfeit actions. God warns us to stay away from such people.

These counterfeit actions may appear Spiritual, but they are not; they are pervaded with flesh. Appearances mean nothing to God – God is concerned with the Source of our actions.

> Deuteronomy 5:29 KJV O that there were such an heart in them, that they would fear Me, and keep all My commandments always, that it might be well with them, and with their children forever!

God is looking for those who have the heart that fears Him and keeps (focuses on, protects, hedges in) His Word.

> Deuteronomy 30:6 NIV The LORD your God will circumcise your hearts and the hearts of your descendants, *so that* you may love Him with all your heart and with all your soul, and live.

We must never forget that this heart that fears God and stays focused on the Word is a gift; we must *receive* this heart. The person who receives this heart is humble; they realize that they need what God is offering and they know that they cannot live without it. They welcome the fact that Spiritual actions cannot be produced without an abundance of the Word. They are not trying to look good; they know they *are* good *in Christ*.

Not only this person experiences the life the Spirit has to offer, but their children do as well. Our decision to walk in the Spirit is a decision that will benefit our entire family. If we want things to "go well" with our family, then we must abide in the Word of God.

If we ignore the Word we are lukewarm. We must realize that being lukewarm is futile.

> Deuteronomy 22:9-11 (NIV) Do not plant two kinds of seed in your vineyard; if you do, not only the crops you plant but also the fruit of the vineyard will be defiled. Do not plow with an ox and a donkey yoked together. Do not wear clothes of wool and linen woven together.

When we are trying to plant Spiritual and carnal seeds at the same time we are working in vain. The crops and the fruit will be defiled – they will be "of the flesh."

An ox and a donkey cannot be put together to work. One is known for strength; the other is often associated with stubbornness and foolishness. The two will not be in agreement in the same way our flesh and our Spirit are not in agreement. Our flesh is foolish; our flesh denies God. No matter how hard we try, the flesh can only produce fruit that denies God. Pairing an ox with a donkey is counterproductive – so is combining our Spirit and our flesh; nothing of value will be produced.

Wool and linen cannot be woven together – wool is heavy and uncomfortable; linen is light, cool, and very comfortable. The law is heavy; grace is comfortable. The Word is our place of repose (Isaiah 28:12); it is our place of relaxation, rest, and dependence upon Christ. When man views the Word as a rule book, he is not in a place of resting in Christ; He is in a place of performance. We cannot view the Word as a rule book and rest in what Christ accomplished for us at the same time.

Mixture is a problem in Christianity – and I am not talking about Christians in relationship with the unsaved. Mixture is Spirit plus flesh.

> 2 Kings 17:32-33, 37-41 NIV They worshiped the LORD, but they also appointed all sorts of their own people to officiate for them as priests in the shrines at the high places. They worshiped the LORD, but they also served their own gods...You must always be careful to keep the decrees and ordinances, the laws and commands He wrote for you. Do not worship other gods. Do not forget the covenant I have made with you, and do not worship other gods. Rather, worship the LORD your God; it is He who will deliver you from the hand of all your enemies. They would not listen, however, but persisted in their former practices. Even while these people were worshiping the LORD, they were serving their idols. To this day their children and grandchildren continue to do as their fathers did.

They worshipped the Lord, BUT...

The word translated here as "worshipped" is the Hebrew word for fear. They feared the Lord, but they did not reverence Him – they did not set Him apart as God. They feared Him – they were around enough to see Him do things that gave them every reason to fear Him, but they did not have a relationship with His Word. They refused to "keep" (focus on, hedge in) the Word that He wrote for them. We must recognize that the Word is *for us*! **Never forget that God's Word is His gift to you; it is His gift of life as He has it!** In refusing to remain focused on His Word, they lived a life of mixture. They knew what the Word said, but they did not regard the Word as their life. They looked at the Word as a rule book they could conquer. They forgot the covenant of faith that God made with them and instead remembered man's covenant of works. They "appeared" to fear the Lord, but they were only looking to the works of their own hands. They were their own idol. They were living a life of mixture. They were living unto themselves; their lives were not focused on God.

> Acts 7:42 AMP But God turned [away from them] and delivered them up to worship and serve the host (stars) of heaven, as it is written in the book of the prophets: Did you [really] offer to Me slain beasts and sacrifices for forty years in the wilderness (desert), O house of Israel?

God told them to listen – the Hebrew word "shama." He told them to take the Word in and make it part of who they were, but they persisted in the works of their own hands. Every action that they performed was about them; they were not living their lives through God. They lived a life of mixture and they taught their children to do the same.

Mixture is only believing part of what the Word says; it is adding man's thoughts to the Word. Mixture corrupts the person who takes part in it. For example: many times we hear God's children boldly declare God's forgiveness of sin only to hear them speak of His judgment in their very next breath. The Word declares that we *are* forgiven for our sin; it is never to be remembered by God again (Hebrews 8:12). If God promises to remember our sins no more, then why do we believe that we will be judged for what we have done wrong when we die? First John tells us that we can have *confidence* on the day of judgment! We must remove the mixture. The Word does tell us that our works will be tried (or judged) by fire; our works will be shown for what they are – Spiritual or of the flesh. Works that were accomplished in the flesh will not last; they will be burned up. We are not being judged for our sin – Jesus Christ, once for all, took care of our sin – our works are simply being shown for what they are, Spirit or flesh. Only those who reject Christ will be judged according to their sins.

Many times man uses mixture in an effort to manipulate and have control over others. If man can convince you that God forgives you, but He is still going to judge you for your sin, that may scare you into making some changes. Many times man will use this fear to influence another's behavior. We must understand; however, that fear is of the flesh. Any actions that fear generates will only be works of the flesh – flesh gives birth to flesh. The appearance of your actions may change, but the source of your actions remains the same. That is why Jesus said if you *look* on a woman with lust in your heart you have committed adultery. It is not just the way something looks on the outside that matters! Only the Word can enable us to utilize the new heart that God has given us.

Mixture causes confusion; confusion is not of God (1 Corinthians 14:33). When we begin to feel ourselves descending into confusion, we can be sure that we are in the flesh. We can escape the flesh by abiding in the Word of

God. When you are confused about a subject in the Word you need to study that subject. Find as many verses as you can on that topic and dig. Keep your focus on what you *know* to be true. If you know that God promises to remember your sins no more, then you can know that judgment for your sins is mixture. We cannot say that God forgives us, *but...*

If we try to combine the Word of God with our carnal thoughts and ideas we will end up with nothing of value.

> Romans 8:13 KJV For if ye live after the flesh, ye shall die: but if ye through the Spirit do mortify the deeds of the body, ye shall live.

Through the Spirit we mortify the deeds of the body – we crush the flesh when we walk in the Spirit. We cannot defeat the flesh apart from the Spirit. We overcome the death of the flesh when we walk in the Spirit – walking in the Spirit is walking in life.

Living after the flesh only produces dead works. We cannot defeat the flesh when we are walking in the flesh.

> Luke 11:17-18 NIV Jesus knew their thoughts and said to them: "Any kingdom divided against itself will be ruined, and a house divided against itself will fall. If Satan is divided against himself, how can his kingdom stand? I say this because you claim that I drive out demons by Beelzebub."

Our flesh is our unholy nature. It is the nature that belongs to the enemy. The flesh will not be defeated by the flesh. The flesh cannot destroy itself. Only the Spirit can overcome the flesh. If we are attempting to overcome our sinful nature on our own we must understand that the end result will forever be failure.

We must come to the point where we make a decision. What covenant are we going to live by?

> 1 Kings 18:21 NIV Elijah went before the people and said, "How long will you waver between two opinions? If the LORD is God, follow Him; but if Baal is God, follow him." But the people said nothing.

Who is God to you? The Hebrew name for God used here is "Elohim." This name for God represents His role as Creator and Judge, the Almighty. Elijah was asking what the people believed about the Lord, the Self-existent one. Did they believe that the Lord was God or did they believe Baal was? Was the Lord their Creator and was He their judge? Was He the Almighty or was it Baal? Baal was a representation of man's works. Baal was an idol, the work of man's hands. If the Lord was their God, they were going to have to make some changes. If the Lord was God then they would have to follow Him. The Hebrew word for "follow" is "halak." This word is defined as: to walk continually, to exercise self, to tread all around. Elijah was telling them that if the Lord was God then they would have to walk in Him – and He is the Word. Elijah was declaring their need to abide in the Word and get to know the Lord if He was going to be their God. If Baal was their god they would then follow him – they would continue to walk in the ways of works; they would continue under the covenant of man.

Elijah told them that they had to make a choice. They would have to stop claiming the Lord as their God when their actions clearly were opposing.

Hosea 10:2 KJV Their heart is divided; now shall they be found faulty: He shall break down their altars, He shall spoil their images.

Their heart was divided; they were deceived. They were living a life in the flesh and they were not producing anything of value in God's estimation. They needed to stop living a double life.

Matthew 6:24 YLT None is able to serve two lords, for either he will hate the one and love the other, or he will hold to the one, and despise the other; ye are not able to serve God and Mammon.

We cannot serve or operate in the flesh and walk in the Spirit simultaneously. We cannot serve the works of our hands and the Lord God. We must make up our minds.

James 1:6-8 KJV But let him ask in faith, nothing wavering. For he that wavereth is like a wave of the sea driven with the wind and tossed. For let not that man think that he shall receive any thing of the Lord. A double minded man [is] unstable in all his ways.

A double-minded man is referring to the person who is trying to operate in the two natures at one time. The word that "double-minded" was translated from means: two spirited, vacillating (of two minds). A double-minded man is a man that attempts to produce Spiritual actions in the flesh.

A double-minded man believes part of the Word and part of his flesh. He is confused; he is unstable. He is not living in the light of the Word.

A double-minded man is not a man that is fighting the battle for his faith.   A double-minded man is defeated; he is not walking in victory.

Mark 9:24 KJV   And straightway the father of the child cried out, and said with tears, "Lord, I believe; help Thou mine unbelief."

This man was in a battle – his Spirit and his flesh were in conflict.   This man spoke out of this war waging inside of him.   Jesus did not rebuke this man; He answered this man.   This man *did* receive from Jesus.

He was not halting between two opinions; he was fighting his flesh.   There will be times when our flesh rises up and fights us, but we can still receive from the Lord. During these times we must go to the Lord for the help we desperately require.   This man cried out to God for help to overcome his unbelief and we must do the same.   We cannot overcome it on our own.

God is not requiring us to be void of the flesh – keep in mind that He left us with our flesh for a reason: He simply wants our flesh to drive us back to Him!   When our flesh sends us crying into the open arms of Jesus, it has done the job God wants it to perform.

We cannot receive from the Lord when we are operating in the flesh.   The flesh takes pride in earning; the Spirit receives.   In man's attempt to produce Spiritual fruit apart from Christ, a spirit of entitlement is birthed.   No longer are we willing to receive; our pride makes us feel worthy.

God created us to walk in unity with the Word.   We are not supposed to ride the fence regarding the Word of God.

We are not able to walk in the flesh and produce Spiritual fruit at the same time. We cannot combine our carnality with our Spiritual nature. One Spiritual truth plus one carnal act will always equal zero – nothing of value.

CHAPTER 4
IT'S NOT ABOUT ME

John 7:18 AMP
He who speaks on his own authority seeks to
win honor for himself. [He whose teaching
originates with himself seeks his own glory.]
But He Who seeks the glory and is eager
for the honor of Him Who sent Him, He is true;
and there is no unrighteousness or
falsehood or deception in Him.

As we begin to understand the Spiritual nature and its origin we also embark on understanding that we cannot take credit for the Spiritual fruit produced in our lives. If what we believe gives *us* glory and honor then we must recognize that this is what the Bible refers to as idolatry. Idolatry can be defined as giving the place in our lives that only God belongs holding to something or someone else. We are giving ourselves the position that only God should hold when we attempt to take credit for Spiritual actions. When we are bragging about what *we* do for God or what *we* refrain from doing for God, we are seeking honor for ourselves.

Matthew 6:33 NIV But seek first His kingdom and His righteousness, and all these things will be given to you as well.

We are supposed to seek *His* righteousness, not try to establish our own. Pride tells us that we can attain a level of righteousness on our own; humility tells us that we are in desperate need of Christ's righteousness. If we speciously believe that we can achieve our own righteousness we will not seek His. We cannot do enough or be good enough to be Spiritual; we must receive this gift from God.

Acts 3:26 NIV When God raised up His servant, He sent Him first to you to bless you by turning each of you from your wicked ways.

We do not turn from our wicked ways, or our flesh, to bless God; He blesses us by turning us from our wicked ways. Too many times this truth gets distorted. Too many times man attempts to take credit for what only God can do.

Isaiah 45:24 AMP Only in the Lord shall one say, I have righteousness (salvation and victory) and strength [to achieve]…

Only in the Lord do we have the ability to have victory over our flesh. Turning from your wicked ways is a gift from God. I cannot claim the ability to have this victory or strength outside of Christ.

Too many Christians are struggling to bless God and they do not realize that all of the works that they are producing are only works of the flesh. We must understand that we cannot impress God or bless Him.

> Isaiah 66:1-2 AMP   Thus says the Lord: Heaven is My throne, and the earth is My footstool. What kind of house would you build for Me? And what kind can be My resting-place?   For all these things My hand has made, and so all these things have come into being [by and for Me], says the Lord. But this is the man to whom I will look and have regard: he who is humble and of a broken or wounded spirit, and who trembles at My word and reveres My commands.

We must keep in mind that everything is about God and everything Spiritual finds its origin in God (John 1:3, Colossians 1:17).   If we understand this we will also understand that we cannot do anything *for* God.

> Job 22:2 AMP   Can a man be profitable to God? Surely he that is wise is profitable to himself.

We cannot be of service to God.   When we are wise we will understand this and we will stop trying to do *for* Him; instead, we will go *to* Him.   He is doing for us when we produce Spiritual fruit.   We must recognize who we are apart from Him.

> Ecclesiastes 3:18 AMP   I said in my heart regarding the subject of the sons of men, God is trying (separating and sifting) them, that they may see that by themselves [under the sun, without God] they are but like beasts.

Apart from Christ we are "but like beasts." There is no mistaking what is being said in this verse. We cannot give ourselves any glory; it all belongs to God.

The Bible tells us that God regards the person who is humble and of a broken spirit. The word translated as "regard" means to look intently at, favor, and regard with pleasure. God is pleased when we are humble, when we understand that apart from Him we can do nothing Spiritual. He is pleased with those who have a broken and wounded spirit. The word translated as "broken and wounded" means hopeless, smitten, lame, and repentant. We must understand that we are hopeless without Christ; there is no hope for Spiritual fruit outside of Christ. We are Spiritually lame on our own; we desperately need Christ. This understanding drives us to the open arms of the Word of God. Trembling at and revering the Word are the result of knowing who we are without Christ.

If we are ignoring the Word it is because we do not understand that the Word is our Spiritual Source. When we disregard the Word we will only produce the fruit of the flesh.

Isaiah 66:3 AMP [The acts of the hypocrite's worship are as abominable to God as if they were offered to idols.] He who kills an ox [then] will be as guilty as if he slew and sacrificed a man; he who sacrifices a lamb or a kid, as if he broke a dog's neck and sacrificed him; he who offers a cereal offering, as if he offered swine's blood; he who burns incense [to God], as if he blessed an idol. [Such people] have chosen their own ways, and they delight in their abominations.

A hypocrite. We usually look at a hypocrite as someone who says one thing and does another. As we study these verses again we find that the hypocrite is the person who tries to produce something Spiritual in their flesh. We recall that God also refers to this type of person as "lukewarm" in Revelation. They try to mix works and grace. They try to accomplish in the flesh what can only be done through Christ. The hypocrite does not focus on the Word and they do not take it in; they are more occupied with works. God tells us that He regards *anything* the hypocrite does as something offensive to Him. What looks right on the outside is not always Spiritual.

God's plan for us is the Word of God; too many times man ignores that plan and tries to produce Spiritual fruit without the Word. When we want to accomplish or perform the Word instead of being empowered *by* the Word, we must understand without a doubt that we are only producing works of the flesh.

> Acts 7:41 HNV They made a calf in those days, and brought a sacrifice to the idol, and rejoiced in the works of their hands.

Too many times we rejoice in the work or *our* hands instead of taking the Word in and letting God do the work in us. **Man can become preoccupied with what he thinks he can achieve; as long as man wants to take any credit they will not live the life that God has available for them.** Again we see the "I do it!" syndrome at work. Anyone who deals with little children understands this problem. How many times do we hear children declare, "I do it!" only to witness them finding themselves incapable. *Every* time we declare "I do it!" we *will* find ourselves incompetent.

God's plan is for us to hear the Word and focus on the Word, to hedge it in and make it part of who we are. We cannot be reminded of this enough. The Word is not for us to try to live up to. The Word is not about rules and regulations; the Word is our life. When we try to produce Spiritual fruit outside of the Word of God it is not pleasing to God; it is detestable to Him. God is not impressed with what we can do outside of Christ. God calls our works of the flesh abominations. The more we are reminded of this, the better. Man needs to *know*, without a doubt, that he is desperate for God.

> Jeremiah 17:5-6 AMP Thus says the Lord: Cursed [with great evil] is the strong man who trusts in and relies on frail man, making weak [human] flesh his arm, and whose mind and heart turn aside from the Lord. For he shall be like a shrub or a person naked and destitute in the desert; and he shall not see any good come, but shall dwell in the parched places in the wilderness, in an uninhabited salt land.

Do you understand that your Spiritual life is not about you? It is all about Christ and what He has done for you. If we put the focus on ourselves we will not produce any fruit of Spiritual value; we will be like that shrub Jeremiah speaks of. We will not see any good come outside of Christ. This is the truth of the Word of God. When we understand this truth we will give God the glory He deserves.

> John 3:21 NIV But whoever lives by the truth comes into the light, so that it may be seen plainly that what he has done has been done through God.

Isaiah 26:12 NIV LORD, You establish peace for us;
all that we have accomplished You have done for us.

All that we have accomplished Spiritually is because
of Christ. We did not do anything Spiritual on our own and
if we are living in the Word of God we will understand that.

Galatians 6:14 AMP But far be it from me to glory
[in anything or anyone] except in the cross of our
Lord Jesus Christ (the Messiah) through Whom the
world has been crucified to me, and I to the world!

Do we glory in what we do? Do we feel like we are a
blessing to God? Do we feel like God would be lost without
us?   These thoughts, and thoughts similar to these, are
detrimental to our Spiritual lives. Too many Christians feel
like they are doing *for* God.

Look at worship, for example. The word "worship"
has been misunderstood to the point that we believe we are
doing something for God when we "worship."   What is
worship – what is worship *according to God*?

Romans 12:1 NIV Therefore, I urge you, brothers, in
view of God's mercy, to offer your bodies as living
sacrifices, holy and pleasing to God--this is your
spiritual act of worship.

WORSHIP: ministration OF GOD.

MINISTRATION: care, support, aid, assistance,
        nurture- OF GOD.

**Worship is being cared for <u>by God</u>, supported <u>by
God</u>, aided <u>by God</u>, assisted <u>by God</u>, and nurtured <u>by</u>**

God; we participate in worship because we are abiding in Him! The phrase, "of God" means belonging to God. **Worship is a Spiritual action with a Spiritual source; worship is "of God."** Worship is not "of man."

Chapter seventeen of Acts told us that God is not served by human hands. The word translated as served in that verse also means worshipped. God is not worshipped by *human* hands; God is worshipped in the Spirit.

Worship will begin with knowing that you are holy and pleasing to God because of Christ. Worship has Christ as the focal point, not man. When we live a life of worship it is because God is merciful (not because we are so wonderful). I can only offer my body as a living sacrifice because of *His* goodness.

The word "offer" is often misunderstood, also. To offer, in these particular verses, means "to stand beside" and it comes from a word that means "to abide." This word does *not* mean to present something to God. Offering has to do with counting on Christ, depending on Him, and seeing yourself "in Him." For us to offer our bodies is for us to abide in Christ and connect ourselves to Him.

A sacrifice is something you surrender to God – we can surrender our everyday lives because God is merciful and He has made us holy and acceptable. We surrender our lives because we understand that we are desperate for Him; we admit our inability and we rely on Him. A correct understanding of who we are in Christ and who we are without Him enables us to surrender ourselves. God calls this is your "reasonable" service.

The word "service" means "worship." The word "reasonable" means "of the Word" It also means rational or logical. When we put the two phrases together, like they read in the Word, we see that "reasonable service" is "of the Word worship;" worship is a Spiritual act that finds its origins in the Word of God. **The phrase "reasonable service" can be correctly translated as "of the Word ministration of God." It is the care, nurture, support, and so on, that we receive from God when we abide in His Word.** We cannot worship in the flesh; worship is Spiritual – it is the fruit of abiding in the Word.

> Exodus 3:12 NIV And God said, "I will be with you. And this will be the sign to you that it is I who have sent you: When you have brought the people out of Egypt, you will worship God on this mountain."

God told Moses that worship was proof that He was with them. We cannot worship without God because worship is Spiritual. **If we are living life in the Word to the degree that we are being cared for, nurtured by, supported by, and aided by God, then we are living a life of worship.**

A person who worships is called a worshipper. Let's find out what a worshipper really is.

> John 4:23 AMP A time will come, however, indeed it is already here, when the true (genuine) worshipers will worship the Father in spirit and in truth (reality); for the Father is seeking just such people as these as His worshipers.

By the original definition, a worshipper is someone who "adores" God. This means that a worshipper is passionate about God. A worshipper is "stuck on God" – they will not wander away from Him; their life is consumed with abiding in Christ – for them to live is Christ. A worshipper is in love with God – and we know that a person only loves Him because He first loved them, so this person knows God is in love with them. They are intimately acquainted with His love.

True worshippers are those Christians who are full of truth (the Word). They worship in Spirit and in truth. The Word is Spirit and the Word is truth – **the true worshipper is abiding in the Word continually**; they are not just singing in a church service. **They are getting the care, support, aid, assistance, and nurture of God because they are abiding in the Word.**

God is looking for the Christian who understands this. When we appreciate this we focus on Christ; we realize that living our everyday life in a Spiritual manner can only be done through Him. We realize that **we cannot offer Him worship – worship is His gift to us!** We have nothing to offer Him – and the sooner we figure that out, the sooner we will become desperate for Him and receive from Him!

> Philippians 3:3 NIV   For it is we who are the circumcision, we who worship by the Spirit of God, who glory in Christ Jesus, and who put no confidence in the flesh.

Circumcision is a sign of the covenant. The covenant is God's promises (1 Chronicles 16:15); it is the Word of God. Only a person who is connected to the Word can worship. We glory (boast) in Christ when we worship – not ourselves; we have zero confidence in our flesh or what we can do apart from Christ when we are true worshippers!

> 2 Corinthians 3:4-5 NIV   Such confidence as this is ours through Christ before God. Not that we are competent in ourselves to claim anything for ourselves, but our competence comes from God.

When we get to the place that we understand we cannot do anything for God on our own that is when we begin to live a life of real worship; a life of "of the Word ministration of God." A life where we are being cared for by God, supported by God, aided by God, assisted by God, and nurtured by God, because we are abiding in Him.

Luke 17:7-10 KJV
"Suppose one of you had a servant plowing
or looking after the sheep. Would he say to the
servant when he comes in from the field, 'Come
along now and sit down to eat'? Would he not
rather say, 'Prepare my supper, get yourself
ready and wait on me while I eat and drink;
after that you may eat and drink'? Would he
thank the servant because he did what he
was told to do? So you also, when you have done
everything you were told to do, should say,
'We are unworthy servants;
we have only done our duty.'"

We must understand that we are unprofitable servants. This means that we are useless. Now before we get offended, let us look at this further. We are useless *on our own*.

How many of us feel like we should be asked to "come and take our place at the table?" On the other hand, how many of us feel like we should be eating *under* the table? Are you trying to earn your spot or are you under the table feeding on crumbs? Either mindset is wrong.

We are told that the servant is not granted a spot at the table for his service – he cannot *earn* his spot. Why? He cannot be worthy of a spot at the table because he is only doing what he was "commanded" to do.

> COMMANDED: to *arrange thoroughly, institute, prescribe,* etc.:-appoint, give, (set in) order, ordain.
> The CHANNEL of an act – not the origination of the act.

The servant does not warrant a spot at the table for what he has done because what he did was actually done *through* his master – if it were not for the master, he could not accomplish what was carried out. We are not the creators of Spiritual fruit; we are the channel of the Spiritual acts. For example, if the master did not have fields there would be no need to harvest. The servant harvests what is owned by the master and he uses what belongs to the master to do so.

> 1 Corinthians 9:7a KJV Who goeth a warfare any time at his own charges?

We cannot produce Spiritual fruit on our own, nor are we expected to. He provides us with everything we need to produce Spiritual fruit. We do not have what we need in and of ourselves and God knows that; that is why He provides for us.
We are not responsible for the Spiritual things we do – Christ THOROUGHLY ARRANGED for us to be the channel through which *He* works! We must understand that we are unworthy servants apart from Christ.

John 15:5 NIV I am the vine; you are the branches. If a man remains in Me and I in him, he will bear much fruit; APART FROM ME YOU CAN DO NOTHING.

We must appreciate that we are "in Him" if we are walking in our Spiritual nature – and *in Him* we find our worth and our ability. *You* are not doing anything for God on your own. You cannot offer Him anything. You cannot sacrifice anything for Him. Anything that is actually Spiritual is *all* because of Him!

In Luke we see that we are only doing our "duty." The word "duty" comes from the word "ophelos" which means to accumulate. It is the accumulation of the Word of God in your heart that produces the Spiritual action in you. Part of the definition of the word translated as duty is "accruing." This refers to something that comes as a result or consequence of something else. Because He is supplying us with everything we need through His Word, we can produce Spiritual fruit. Abiding in the Word *results* in Spiritual actions. **It is nothing that *we* do that results in Spiritual actions; it is the work that the Word does in us.**

When you understand the Word and store the Word inside of you, it *will* come back out. We are only doing what has been stored up in us…His Word. Even our love for Him is because of His love for us! We cannot even love Him on our own.

1 John 4:19 NIV We love because He first loved us.

We must be dependent on His love for us; we must rely on it and not on ourselves.

Matthew 6:26 NIV Look at the birds of the air; they do not sow or reap or store away in barns, and yet your heavenly Father feeds them. Are you not much more valuable than they?

If birds (who have less value than we do) do not have to do something in order to be taken care of, why would we think that we have to? Why would we rely on what we can do when even the birds do not?

The concept of the law taught working to earn, but the covenant of faith did not. *Man* tells us that we have to try to earn something from God – *not God*!

Job 12:7 AMP For ask now the animals, and they will teach you [that God does not deal with His creatures according to their character]; ask the birds of the air, and they will tell you.

Animals are more intelligent than we are in some aspects! Ask the birds; look at their example. Why does God take care of them? He takes care of them because they are His creation and He loves them! He takes responsibility for them; they are His!

He is not taking care of them because they worked hard enough. They do not eat because they planted their food. The Bible tells us to ask and they will "tell;" to tell means to expose; stand boldly out opposite; praise. If we just consider the animals we will see the lie of works is exposed! Their lives boldly declare the opposite of the theory that teaches working to earn from God. When this lie is exposed *God* gets the praise – *He* is the Supplier and Sustainer! When we beyond doubt understand this, all we can be is thankful!

When we mistakenly believe that we have to earn God's promises then we also believe we deserve some glory – after all, "we" did what needed to be done. This is a devious ploy of the enemy – he wants us to believe that our actions produce the things we desire. Words like "obedience" are used and then we think that surely there is something to this. We need to know unquestionably that only faith can produce Spiritual fruit in us – faith that comes from the Word of God (Romans 10:17)! Any fruit that we can produce outside of Christ is fugacious and futile; it is only temporary and it has no value.

It is fundamental to identify with the fact that we are Spiritually impotent without Christ. God does not owe us thanks; He cannot be indebted to us. When we understand the truth we will then find ourselves thanking Him for what His Word does in our lives instead of expecting He owes us.

> Philippians 2:13 AMP [Not in your own strength] for it is God Who is all the while effectually at work in you [energizing and creating in you the power and desire], both to will and to work for His good pleasure and satisfaction and delight.

Even your *desire* to do something Spiritual cannot be accredited to you! Our confidence must be properly placed in Christ alone.

> 2 Corinthians 4:7 NIV But we have this treasure in jars of clay to show that this all-surpassing power is from God and not from us.

I have nothing in which to boast when I understand who I am apart from Christ. I have no reason to believe that God is in debt to me for actions that I have performed.

In Matthew, chapter twenty, we see a parable about workers. These workers were complaining about their wages. They were hired at the beginning of the day and they agreed to the amount they would work for. Later on, however, other workers were hired. These other workers only worked a fraction of the time compared to those hired first, but these workers were still paid the same wage. We can learn something from this parable. It does not matter how much we do. No one was better or deserved more than another because of how much they did. The Bible tells us that it was "just" to give them the same pay. All of the workers received what was just or fair. Without the owner of the field, none of them would have been able to do anything. It was only because of him that they could do the work and they received what was just based on the owner, not based on what they did.

On our own, we are unprofitable servants – that is why He no longer calls us servants. God recognizes us according to who we are in Christ.

> John 15:14-16 KJV   Ye are My friends, if ye do whatsoever I command you. Henceforth I call you not servants; for the servant knoweth not what his lord doeth: but I have called you friends; for all things that I have heard of My Father I have made known unto you. Ye have not chosen Me, but I have chosen you, and ordained you, that ye should go and bring forth fruit, and [that] your fruit should remain: that whatsoever ye shall ask of the Father in My name, He may give it you.

A servant does not know his master's business; a slave is not aware of what his master does. The master keeps his business to himself; he does not share it with his servants. God does not look at us as servants. He looks at us as friends or associates; a friend is the person who is connected with Christ.

We are His friends if we do what He says. How do we do what He says? **Spiritual actions are only the end result of storing up the Word inside of us.** He tells us we are friends because we hear what the Father says – faith comes from hearing the Word and that faith will eventually produce Spiritual actions. We are friends – we are empowered by the Word; we are connected with Christ. The servant does not know what the Father says; they are not taking the Word in. **The servant is lacking the Word while the friend is full of the Word and his actions confirm that fullness.**

The friend relies on the Word of God; they do not depend on themselves. Jesus declares that He "ordained" us. This word "ordained" comes from a word that means to place in a passive position. Our flesh must be in an inactive position if we are ever going to accomplish the Spiritual. Our flesh cannot be active at the same time our Spirit is active. Now, because of what Christ has provided for us, we can ignore the flesh and we can walk in the Spirit. We can connect with Christ and disconnect from the flesh. The work that Christ has done in us is amazing!

We are also told in these verses, in the fifteenth chapter of John, that we did not choose Christ. This can make some believe that free-will does not exist. That is not what Jesus is saying to us. The Bible declares that Jesus was the Lamb that was slain from the *foundation* of the world; He chose to die for everyone *before* anyone chose to accept Him; and in doing so, He chose everyone. His sacrifice is available to all. If Jesus Christ would not have chosen us first, we would not have been able to receive Him. We did not initiate the death of Christ; He did. We do not set ourselves apart like some teach. I am set apart in Christ. He ordained us; He set us apart; He chose us.

I need to see myself according to who I am in Jesus Christ. I am a joint-heir with Him; everything that He has is available to me, also. I am at peace with God; the Father is pleased with Jesus; therefore, the Father is pleased with me. Jesus is the beloved Son; for that reason, I am a beloved child of God, too. Everything that Jesus has is also ours; it is ours thanks to Jesus! We are legal inheritors; we have the right to all that is ours in Christ.

We do not have to fall for the lies that say God is not pleased with us or we do not have what we need. We can know that God is pleased with us because of Christ! We can know that we have available to us every last thing we will ever need. Our new identity secures God's approval; Jesus Christ purchased the approval of God for me and He provided me with everything I will ever need through His precious promises (2 Peter 1:3-4). I had nothing to do with it; I am simply a beneficiary!

We are co-workers with Christ. We have available to us everything that Christ has available to Him and we are well-able to produce Spiritual fruit.

> Romans 8:16-17a   KJV   The Spirit itself beareth witness with our spirit, that we are the children of God: And if children, then heirs; heirs of God, and joint-heirs with Christ.

We are joint-heirs with Christ! Why do we continue to believe that we are lacking? What belongs to Him, belongs to us! We must rise up and take our rightful place in Christ. Why would we continue to live like a servant when

He calls us friends? If we recall the prodigal son, we can see this principal being taught yet again. The son wanted to come back to his father and work as a servant, but the father would not give his consent. Our Father is not in agreement with us living a life as a servant. He longs for us to take our rightful position as a joint-heir with Christ.

As long as we view ourselves as servants we will also view our actions as works. Our works result from *our* effort and exertion, not from Christ working through us. God does not need what our flesh can produce.

> Acts 17:24-25 NIV The God who made the world and everything in it is the Lord of heaven and earth and does not live in temples built by hands. And He is not served by human hands, as if He needed anything, because He Himself gives all men life and breath and everything else.

We cannot persist in believing that we are serving God or doing Him a favor when we continue to see what the Word is boldly declaring. **Everything Spiritual we have and everything we do Spiritually is only because of Him.** We are not giving Him anything!

> 1 Chronicles 29:14 NIV "But who am I, and who are my people, that we should be able to give as generously as this? Everything comes from You, and we have given You only what comes from Your hand."

Pride leads us to believe that we are accomplishing something for God; humility understands that this is simply not possible.

Any fruit that we produce on our own is of no Spiritual value. Why continue to produce worthless works when we could be producing Spiritual fruit through Christ that lasts for eternity?

> 1 Corinthians 15:58 KJV ...be ye steadfast, unmovable, always abounding in the work of the Lord, forasmuch as ye know that your labor is not in vain in the Lord.

We must realize what we have in Christ. In realizing this we will be unmovable – we will remain in the Word. As we abide in the Word we will find ourselves abounding in God's work instead of our own works, and we know that whatever we do through Christ lasts forever.

When we are producing fruit belonging to the flesh it is in vain; only what we do through Christ has eternal value.

Our "labor in the Lord" is the Spiritual actions we produce as the result of continuing in the Word. When we are convinced that those actions are only accomplished because of Him, then we will give the glory to Him.

> Psalms 115:1 NIV Not to us, O LORD, not to us but to Your name be the glory, because of Your love and faithfulness.

His love and faithfulness provide us with everything we need to have a Spiritual identity. We can only produce Spiritual fruit when we are in agreement with this identity. As we focus on the work that Christ has done in us, we will begin to understand clearly that He is serving us; we are not serving Him.

CHAPTER 6

TWO KINDS OF LOVE

1 John 4:19 NIV
We love because He first loved us.

Love is such a small word but it boasts such great meaning.
Love must be understood by us if we are ever going to truly
love. Looking over the above verse, we see that we are only
capable of love after we first receive God's love. We need to
be loved by God.

> Song of Solomon 1:4 NIV Take me away with You--
> let us hurry! Let the King bring me into His
> chambers. We rejoice and delight in You; we will
> praise Your love more than wine. How right they are
> to adore You!

Take me away, Jesus, and take me quickly! We need
to quickly get alone with God. Let Him take you into His
presence – abide in the Word. Go to that quiet place, that
place of shelter and love that only Christ can provide. When
we get alone with God and let Him love on us something
happens – we rejoice. We are overwhelmed with His love
and all we can do is rejoice!

> REJOICE: brighten up. To cause or make to be full
> of glee (delight, hilarity, excitement, joy).
> Cheer up. Very.

DELIGHT / BE GLAD: to spin around because of
aggressive emotion (usually the emotion of
joy).

Both of the above definitions describe what the love
of God can do for us. There are too many Christians running
low on God's love for them.

Christians are meant to be bright and cheerful. This is
God's plan for us.

Psalms 34:5 AMP They looked to Him and were
radiant; their faces shall never blush for shame or be
confused.

Looking to Him makes us radiant. It makes us
sparkle; it makes us cheerful.

If we are going to walk this out, then it will only be
because we are intimately familiar with the love of God that
is in Christ Jesus. Part of the definition for the word that
"radiant" was translated from means: to flow, from the sheen
of a running stream. When we are focused on Christ He is
flowing through us and we are radiant! We sparkle and the
world cannot help but to notice.

As we look to Christ, praise is inevitable. A life that
is focused on Him will be a life of praise. As we focus on
Christ we begin to see mounting reasons to praise Him. We
will praise or remember His love more than wine.

PRAISE / REMEMBER: to mark so as to be
recognized. Consider, mention, be mindful of.
Think on. Make to be remembered.

MORE THAN: among. A part of. Because of. Above.

> WINE: intoxication (under the influence, to make intensely excited or overjoyed). Effervesce (to be lively; high spirited or excited). Banqueting.

We can mark His love by the intense feelings it produces. If we are feeling beat up, depressed, guilty, and so forth, then we can know that we are not under the influence of His love. His love is found among extreme joy and liveliness!

> Habakkuk 3:17-18 NIV Though the fig tree does not bud and there are no grapes on the vines, though the olive crop fails and the fields produce no food, though there are no sheep in the pen and no cattle in the stalls, yet I will rejoice in the LORD, I will be joyful in God my Savior.

As we focus on His love we are able to praise Him even during hard times. It is important for us to be able to rejoice even when we are in an "off-season" in life. Remember that we will only do this when we are abiding in His love – we must be mindful of His love! When we are focusing on our circumstances we will find rejoicing elusive. Taking the focus off of Christ's love for us can lead us into fear. If we are not convinced of His love for us we can fall into the trap of believing that we are suffering in a trial because God is mad at us and He is punishing us. Remind yourself of His love; fill up on verses that proclaim His never-ending love for you.

The Word tells us to praise His love more than wine. Wine can also mean banqueting.

Song of Solomon 2:4 KJV He brought me to the banqueting house, and His banner over me [was] love.

The word for banqueting is the same Hebrew word for wine. If we look at the Hebrew spelling for these words, we see that we get to this place of being under the influence of His love by humility. When we find ourselves in this place, this is real life – this is Spiritual living; it is life as God has it!

Jude 1:20 MSG …staying right at the center of God's love, keeping your arms open and outstretched, ready for the mercy of our Master, Jesus Christ. This is the unending life, the real life!

We will find that keeping ourselves surrounded by God's love enables us to enjoy a Spiritual life. We need to keep ourselves open to His love; we need to be ready to receive. Are you ready to receive? Are you keeping your arms open? Are you ready for mercy? Mercy is God reaching out to meet our needs in spite of us. Do you believe that God wants to help you even though you struggle with your flesh? Do you expect mercy or do you expect judgment?

1 John 4:17 KJV Herein is our love made perfect, that we may have boldness in the day of judgment: because as He is, so are we in this world.

Love is made complete (or perfect) when we see ourselves in Christ. When we know who we are, love is accomplished – it has done its job. The love of Christ is what reveals who we really are in Him.

Nothing but love can give a new identity to depraved humanity. Nothing but love can give us boldness in the "day of judgment."

"In the day of judgment" denotes a period of time – it can mean forever or always. You may judge yourself daily and we know that others will judge you, but we must understand that the only judgment that counts has already been made – we have been found innocent in Christ. **Because of what Christ has done for us, we are forever and always innocent!** When we are in agreement with God's verdict of "not guilty in Christ," we will regard judging ourselves and others as a worthless endeavor. We will also be able to disregard the judgment others place on us. Understanding the two natures leaves us with no reason to scrutinize.

> 1 Corinthians 4:3-4 NIV I care very little if I am judged by you or by any human court; indeed, I do not even judge myself. My conscience is clear, but that does not make me innocent. It is the Lord who judges me.

Only the love of God can forgive and forget! We are told that we can have boldness or assurance in regards to judgment because He has loved us enough to give us *His* identity!

> Colossians 3:3 NIV For you died, and your life is now hidden with Christ in God.

Life is found in Christ. We must identify with who we are because of Him. His love for us gives us life; it gives us a new identity.

Romans 7:4 NIV So, my brothers, you also died to the law through the body of Christ, that you might belong to another, to Him who was raised from the dead, in order that we might bear fruit to God.

We belong to another when we accept His sacrifice for us. This means we are "married to" another. Before we received Christ we belonged to the devil (and our flesh still does).

Ephesians 2:1-5 NIV As for you, you were dead in your transgressions and sins, in which you used to live when you followed the ways of this world and of the ruler of the kingdom of the air, the spirit who is now at work in those who are disobedient. All of us also lived among them at one time, gratifying the cravings of our sinful nature and following its desires and thoughts. Like the rest, we were by nature objects of wrath. But because of His great love for us, God, who is rich in mercy, made us alive with Christ even when we were dead in transgressions--it is by grace you have been saved.

We live according to the flesh when we follow (be occupied with, be a companion of) the ways of the flesh. Because of the great love God has for us, we can now follow (be occupied with, be a companion of) the ways of the Spirit. We can live the real life because of His great love for us.

We see in Romans that we can also "bear fruit *to* God" because of His love for us. What does this mean? In studying this verse, we discover that the word "to" is not in the original translation. It literally means bearing God fruit – or the fruit of God. We can produce Spiritual fruit because of the love God has for us. We have the ability to participate in the Divine nature (2 Peter 1:4) every day and produce Spiritual fruit as a result of the love God has for us. This is what we continually have available to us because of who we are in Christ!

His love has blessed us infinitely. What do you know about the love God has for you?

We see in the Word that His love is everlasting – nothing we can do and nothing we go through can change that!

> Jeremiah 31:3-4 NIV   The LORD appeared to us in the past, saying: "I have loved you with an everlasting love; I have drawn you with loving-kindness. I will build you up again and you will be rebuilt..."

> BUILD: to build; to repair. Obtain children.
>   Make; set (up); surely.

The Hebrew spelling for the word translated as "build" shows us that we necessitate the Seed if we are going to be repaired, put together, fruitful, and secure. The Seed is the center of having Jesus as our Master and receiving His power; the Seed is the center of producing fruit and praising God for it. The Seed is the Word of God (Luke 8:11, 1 Peter 1:23).

Understand that God loves you and that He is not angry with you. Open your eyes to everything God's Word says about His love for you. He is not angry; anger does not describe God's feelings for you. The Word tells us that anger is cruel and overwhelming. This does not describe our God.

Also remember that God's anger is righteous; it is for the unsaved – not us!   It would not be righteous if God were to be angry with us for the sin that Christ already paid the price for. Jesus Christ took that anger and wrath upon Himself for us; we no longer have to fear it.

The Bible describes love in First Corinthians. Chapter thirteen tells us that love is patient; so, we can conclude that God is patient because God is love. The many facets of love describe our Savior. We also see that God does not hold our sin against us because love does not keep a record of wrongs. If love does not keep a record of wrongs, then God does not keep a record of wrongs. We can trust in His love instead of fearing His anger.

> Lamentations 3:21 NIV Yet this I call to mind and therefore I have hope: Because of the Lord's great love we are not consumed, for His compassions never fail. They are new every morning; great is Your faithfulness.

His great love is what we need to "call to mind;" we need to think on His love for us. His great love gives us hope; it gives us the ability to wait, trust, and expect! We never have to worry about the past, today, or the future, when we are abiding in His love.

God's faithfulness is great. It is abundant; there is more than enough for me! If I ever feel like I am lacking faithfulness then I need to focus on His faithfulness. Anything that puts the focus on you is "of the flesh." Walk in the Spirit; put the focus on Christ, where it belongs. If I feel like I do not love God enough, then I need to focus more on His love for me! Spiritual love and faithfulness are *not* about me!

1 John 4:10 NIV   This is love: NOT that we loved God, but that He loved us and sent His Son as an atoning sacrifice for our sins.

There is something very interesting about love in the Hebrew language. When we are told to "love" God it is the Hebrew word "ahab." This word means to have affection for; love; like. It is masculine; a masculine word denotes that it is not fruit-bearing.

The Hebrew spelling for this love we have for God articulates to us that love is the connection between God and man.   We are connected by grace – the Word and its influence in our daily lives connects us to God. Uniting with God in this way makes Him the Master of our house and it releases His power!

We see something different when we look at the word used for the love God has for us. When the Word talks of His love for us it is the Hebrew word "ahabah." This word means the same thing as "ahab" except it is the feminine form of the word – it *is* fruit-bearing!

Our love for God does not produce Spiritual fruit! It is His love for us that produces the Spiritual fruit! It is all about Him! He deserves all the praise! It is critical that we understand this. There can be no confusion regarding this precept.

John 14:15 KJV   If ye love Me, keep My commandments.

John 15:10 KJV If ye keep My commandments, ye shall abide in My love; even as I have kept My Father's commandments, and abide in His love.

We must not forget the true meaning of what was translated as the word "keep." **To keep His commandments does not mean to never sin; to keep His commandments means to remain focused on the Word.**

We must also remember that we only love Him because He first loved us. In remembering these two vital precepts, we will understand what the above verses really mean and we will not be confused. If we love God it is only because He first loved us and this love will lead us to the Word. We will keep our eyes on the Word, we will focus on the Word, and we will protect the Word in our lives when we walk in the love God has for us. Remaining in the Word *is* remaining in His love.

When we look at the Hebrew spelling for both words for love, we find one extra letter "hey" in this word that describes God's love for us. The letter hey represents grace. Grace, we recall, is the Divine influence in our daily lives. This reveals to us that God loves us through the Word. The Word is our source; it is the *one* thing! The one thing important enough to mention twice in the spelling of the Hebrew word for God's Love for us! When we are hedging the Word of God in our lives we are abiding in love; He is the Word and He is love.

There is never a time for us to try to earn from God! If we misconstrue what God is articulating and try to produce more love for God or try to make ourselves more faithful, we will fail.

We must keep the focus where it belongs: on Christ and His undying love for us.

CHAPTER 7

GETTING TO KNOW YOU

Philippians 3:8-11 NIV
What is more, I consider everything a loss compared to the surpassing greatness of knowing Christ Jesus my Lord, for whose sake I have lost all things. I consider them rubbish, that I may gain Christ and be found in Him, not having a righteousness of my own that comes from the law, but that which is through faith in Christ--the righteousness that comes from God and is by faith. I want to know Christ and the power of His resurrection and the fellowship of sharing in His sufferings, becoming like Him in His death, and so, somehow, to attain to the resurrection from the dead.

Ephesians 1:18-20 KJV
I pray also that the eyes of your heart may be enlightened in order that you may know the hope to which He has called you, the riches of His glorious inheritance in the saints, and His incomparably great power for us who believe. That power is like the working of His mighty strength, which He exerted in Christ when He raised Him from the dead and seated Him at His right hand in the heavenly realms...

If we are going to discover and walk in our new identity, then we are going to have to get to know Christ to a greater extent.

We will get to know Him more and more as we abide in the Word. We will have the eyes of our heart enlightened when we believe – and, remember, we believe because we abide in the Word. Abiding in the Word produces power – the same power God used to raise Christ from the dead. Abiding in the Word must be our way of life.

If we are going to know the hope we have concerning resurrection power we must remain in the Word. Every good thing we desire is going to come from the Word. You have resurrection power in you because of Christ. Tap into it! Abide in the Word concerning the power that is yours.

> Ephesians 2:4-7 NIV But because of His great love for us, God, who is rich in mercy, made us alive with Christ even when we were dead in transgressions--it is by grace you have been saved. And God raised us up with Christ and seated us with Him in the heavenly realms in Christ Jesus, in order that in the coming ages He might show the incomparable riches of His grace, expressed in His kindness to us in Christ Jesus.

Resurrection power lives inside of us; we have been made alive in Christ! This means that we are Spiritual beings now – but do not forget that we still have our flesh, as well. We cannot be reminded enough regarding the fact that Christ loves us so much that He took our sin and paid for it so that we could be alive in Him. His love for us has provided us with a new identity.

This love He has for me is a testimony to others. He wants to show who He is and how He loves the world, and He wants to do it *through* us! When others see us living a resurrected (Spiritual) life it is a testimony to the kindness of God and the riches of His grace.

Romans 6:4-11 NIV We were therefore buried with Him through baptism into death in order that, just as Christ was raised from the dead through the glory of the Father, we too may live a new life. If we have been united with Him like this in His death, we will certainly also be united with Him in His resurrection. For we know that our old self was crucified with Him so that the body of sin might be done away with, that we should no longer be slaves to sin because anyone who has died has been freed from sin. Now if we died with Christ, we believe that we will also live with Him. For we know that since Christ was raised from the dead, He cannot die again; death no longer has mastery over Him. The death He died, He died to sin once for all; but the life He lives, He lives to God. In the same way, count yourselves dead to sin but alive to God in Christ Jesus.

Here we see the gift of a new life, again. This new life is realized when we understand what Christ did for us. He died and rose for us – are you in agreement with this? I am not asking if you believe this in the minimal sense. I am asking you if you are in agreement with this according to God's definition of agreement. According to God, if you are in agreement with something it is being displayed in your life. Does your life display Spiritual life?

His death gives us the power we need to overcome our flesh (death) and live this Spiritual (resurrected) life. When we understand that He defeated the flesh we will no longer live as slaves to it. If we are living as a slave to sin it is only because we are not walking in our new identity.

Christ was raised from the dead – He defeated death for me and you. In defeating death He defeated sin – the wages of sin is death; if we are free from sin's power we are free from death.

> 1 Corinthians 15:56-57 NIV The sting of death is sin, and the power of sin is the law. But thanks be to God! He gives us the victory through our Lord Jesus Christ.

We can now live a life that is dead to sin and alive to God; through Christ we have victory over death and sin. He defeated death, sin, and the grave at the cross. He paid the price that we could not pay. He has dealt with the sin problem of man and it is finished.

> Hebrews 9:28 AMP Even so it is that Christ, having been offered to take upon Himself and bear as a burden the sins of many once and once for all, will appear a second time, not to carry any burden of sin nor to deal with sin, but to bring to full salvation those who are [eagerly, constantly, and patiently] waiting for and expecting Him.

Sin has been taken care of once for all. No longer do we need to fear the punishment or the death that our sin deserves. Christ has paid the price in full; in Him we are free from sin and its penalty.
We must "count" or consider ourselves dead to sin and alive to God in Christ. We need to see ourselves based on who we are in Christ. We need to stop identifying ourselves based on who we are outside of Christ.

> Romans 5:1 AMP Therefore, since we are justified (acquitted, declared righteous, and given a right

standing with God) through faith, let us [grasp the fact that we] have [the peace of reconciliation to hold and to enjoy] peace with God through our Lord Jesus Christ (the Messiah, the Anointed One).

Take hold of your new identity; see yourself in Christ. You have resurrection power inside of you – you have the power you need to live a life that is Spiritual if you focus on your identity in Christ (by abiding in the Word of God).

In knowing Christ we also experience sharing in His sufferings. What does the phase, found in the third chapter of Philippians, "the fellowship of His suffering" mean? Too many do not understand this phrase; and because of this, they are enduring things they should be conquering.

Sharing in His suffering is referring to the battle of Spirit versus flesh.

Luke 22:42-44 KJV   Saying, Father, if Thou be willing, remove this cup from Me: nevertheless not My will, but Thine, be done. And there appeared an angel unto Him from heaven, strengthening Him. And being in an agony He prayed more earnestly: and His sweat was as it were great drops of blood falling down to the ground.

We know that we have two natures; seeing this, we will also have to recognize the competition that will take place between these two natures.

We share in His suffering when our Spirit and our flesh do battle, in other words, when we engage in Spiritual warfare.

Romans 7:22-23 NIV For in my inner being I delight in God's law; but I see another law at work in the members of my body, waging war against the law of my mind…

There is a war going on inside of us – our Spirit and our flesh are in a battle. We are sharing in His suffering when we engage in this conflict in the same way He did. Jesus' flesh did battle with His Spirit; His flesh did not want to go to the cross.

Each nature wants control; each nature wants things its way. A battle ensues because of this and the battle is for territory. We have 2 parts to each one of us – which one is going to dominate? Which one will we give possession of our territory to?

The flesh hates God and the things of God. The flesh loves death. This truth is sometimes hard to swallow; but nevertheless, it is still truth. Your flesh hates God. Your flesh hates the things of God. The only method of defeating the flesh is the Spiritual nature Christ died to give us.

The flesh does not comprehend life or the Spirit. Our flesh cannot take hold of the Spiritual. That is why something new had to take place inside of us when we received Christ. If we are going to take possession of what Christ has for us, we are going to have to walk in the Spirit.

John 6:63 KJV It is the spirit that quickeneth; the flesh profiteth nothing: the words that I speak unto you, [they] are spirit, and [they] are life.

QUICKENETH: to (re-) *vitalize*. Make alive, give life, quicken –come to life; begin a period of development.

The Holy Spirit of God resides in the believer and gives life. We are brought to Spiritual life through the Word of God. The Word is Spirit and the Word is life. If we are ever going to develop Spiritually, then we are going to have to agree that the Word is our only Source of development.

We cannot achieve anything Spiritual in our flesh. If we are going to win this battle of Spirit versus flesh, then we must be in agreement with the Word. This means that we are going to have to set our minds on the Word. What does Romans, chapter eight, mean when it instructs us to set our mind on things above?

> MINDS SET ON: to exercise the mind, that is, entertain or have an attitude or opinion; by implication to be (mentally) disposed to interest oneself in. Set the affection on, be of the same mind.

What kind of exercise is your mind getting? Spiritual or carnal? What are you reading, watching, thinking about, and so forth, the majority of the time? Are you mentally disposed to the Spirit or the flesh? Are you in agreement with God's Word or the lies that your flesh tells you?

Are you Spiritually minded? Your mind needs to be occupied with the Word of God; if not, you are going to walk in the flesh.

> Romans 12:2a NIV Do not conform any longer to the pattern of this world, but be transformed by the renewing of your mind.

Our minds will experience transformation when they are set on the things of the Spirit. If we ignore the Word and do not set our minds on it, we will continue to walk in the flesh. We need this transformation. Our minds need to associate with Christ.

Our minds are part of the territory being fought for in this Spiritual battle. Satan, in a furtive attempt to gain this territory, will entice us with thoughts that do not agree with the Word. We have authority; we determine what goes in and what goes out. Our minds are not free for the taking. **Only you can choose what you will think on.** Will you be of the same mind as the Spirit? Will you entertain the Word? Will you ignore the flesh or will you give it your time? This is all up to you. God has given you the power to get rid of thoughts that do not agree with His Word. He has given you the Word; the Word is your power. The Word is your avenue to know God better.

As we continue in the Word we find ourselves more familiar with Christ and this leads to becoming like Him in His death.

> 2 Corinthians 5:14-15 NIV For Christ's love compels us, because we are convinced that One died for all, and therefore all died. And He died for all, that those who live should no longer live for themselves but for Him who died for them and was raised again.

> COMPEL: constrains; unites us; to *hold together*, to *compress* or *arrest* (a prisoner); *(to force)*, *preoccupy:* - hold back, keep in, be taken with, throng.

Knowing Christ means knowing His love. Staying focused on the love of Christ unites us with Him. Focusing on His love holds us together – we are no longer falling apart Spiritually because of guilt, condemnation, and the like. His love imprisons us – it keeps us in the Word; it keeps us in the new nature. We are "taken with" His love the more attentive we are to it!

These verses also tell us that we should not live "for ourselves." This phrase comes from one word that means "alone." Its root word means "baffling wind and going backwards." We no longer have to live a life alone or apart from Christ because He loves us.

> Psalms 51:4 KJV   Against thee, thee only, have I sinned, and done [this] evil in thy sight: that thou mightest be justified when thou speakest, [and] be clear when thou judgest.

This verse tells us *why* we find ourselves in sin. "Against thee, thee only," was translated from one Hebrew word: "bad." This word means "separated or alone." Alone, or separated from God, David sinned.   David truly understood why he found himself in sin.   David did not blame his sin on God.   He realized that his sin was the result of separating from God.   The words "justified" and "clear" both refer to being innocent.   We are only innocent because of what Christ did for us.   When we live separated from His love we are choosing the flesh.   We are choosing to live a backward, baffling life.

Concentrate on His love; live united with Christ and move forward.   We can see progress in life because His love paid the price for our advancement.   Bear in mind that when we focus on ourselves we are doing nothing but going backward.

Becoming like Him in His death is seeing ourselves in Christ and not according to our flesh.   How do you see yourself?   We no longer have to regard ourselves from a worldly point of view – we no longer have to recognize ourselves according to the sinful nature (2 Corinthians 5:14-21). Our sin is no longer counted against us when we are in Christ.

We should also teach others to see themselves in Christ. We *have been* reconciled! This means we *have been* made different – we have a new nature; we have the very nature of God living inside of us! We can live a resurrected life when we are walking in the new nature.

> John 1:4-5 KJV In Him was life; and the life was the light of men. And the light shineth in darkness; and the darkness comprehended it not.

We are not going to find life outside of Christ – He *is* life! The more we come to know Him, the more we come to experience life.

The word translated as life in these verses is not referring to eternal life; this is not referring to a home in heaven. Christ is referring to something we can have here and now – life as God has it.

If you look at the definition of life in an English dictionary you will find that it is defined as: "the ability to take in food, adapt to an environment, grow, and reproduce." We can relate this to the Spiritual realm. We take in the Word and *it* gives us what we need to adjust to our circumstances, *it* gives us what we need to grow, and *it* gives us what we need to be productive. The Word is our life! We are not going to experience victorious, Spiritual living without it!

In Him is life. When we live our lives in Christ we are experiencing life; life as God has it! His life is light.

LIGHT: to *shine* or make *manifest*, especially by *rays*;

(compare to show or make known one's thoughts); *luminousness*: - fire.

When we live that "Zoë life" we are expressing who God is. When we live in Christ we will shine. This means we will show, demonstrate, be evidence for, and let others see Christ.

It is Christ in us that brings us to life. When we are walking in the Spirit we are enjoying "Zoë life." Walk in the Spirit – abide in the Word and get in agreement with the Word. The Word of God is what takes us into that life that only God can give!

When we are walking in the flesh we are producing death – nothing of lasting value.

John 8:12 KJV   Then spake Jesus again unto them, saying, I am the light of the world: he that followeth Me shall not walk in darkness, but shall have the light of life.

Jesus tells us that He is the light of the world. He came to display God to the world.

John 14:9 NIV   Jesus answered: "Don't you know Me, Philip, even after I have been among you such a long time? Anyone who has seen Me has seen the Father. How can you say, Show us the Father?"

When we walk in the Spirit we are also displaying God to the world. If we follow Him we will display the Light.

FOLLOWETH: a *road*); properly to *be in the same way with*, that is, to *accompany* (specifically as a disciple): - pursue, reach.

Following Christ is nothing more than being a disciple or a student of the Word. The more we are abiding in the Word, the more we display who He is. Our actions, our thoughts, our feelings, and so on, become like His *when* we remain in the Word of God. **I cannot make myself a disciple; I can only become a disciple because of what I do with the Word of God.** We can be a shining example of Christ to this world if we would only recognize the Word as our Zoë life.

God has given us His heart in the form of the written Word. What are you going to do with it? Are you using the Word and getting to know Christ or are you more familiar with your flesh than you are with your Savior? We are never going to become intimately acquainted with God if we are not intimately acquainted with the Word; He is the Word.

Luke 13:6-9 NIV
Then He told this parable:
"A man had a fig tree, planted in his vineyard,
and he went to look for fruit on it, but did not find any.
So he said to the man who took care of the vineyard,
'For three years now I've been coming to look for fruit on
this fig tree and haven't found any. Cut it down!
Why should it use up the soil?'
"'Sir,' the man replied, 'leave it alone for one more year,
and I'll dig around it and fertilize it. If it bears fruit next
year, fine! If not, then cut it down.'"

We can look at the born again child of God as this tree in the book of Luke. God wants His children to grow and produce fruit.

> John 15:8 NIV This is to My Father's glory, that you bear much fruit, showing yourselves to be My disciples.

God is glorified (rendered glorious or esteemed as glorious) when we show ourselves to be His disciples or His students. A student becomes like his teacher; a student takes on the characteristics of their teacher. As students of the Word of God, we will produce the same fruit as *the* Teacher.

If we have been born again, but we are not producing fruit, then there is some work that needs to be done in our lives.

The vinedresser told the owner that he would "dig" around the tree. When you dig around a tree, you create empty space. You remove the soil that is not fostering the tree. In getting rid of that useless soil, you are making room for something that *will* nourish and promote growth in the tree. Digging gets rid of what is sapping the life out of the tree. Can you relate?

What is sapping the life out of you? What needs to go in your life? Anything in your life that agrees with your flesh needs to go! Simply realizing that something needs to go is not enough – we must get rid of what needs to go and we must then fill that space with something that promotes life, something Spiritual.

We can look at negative thoughts as an example. We may realize that we think negative thoughts, but what we do about these thoughts is what matters. When I realize that I am thinking negative thoughts, I need to "dig" and replace. It is not enough to get rid of these thoughts, we must replace these thoughts with what the Word of God says about our thoughts. We must replace the lie with the truth; we must replace the flesh with the Spirit. If we do not replace the thoughts of the flesh, these thoughts will quickly find their way back (Matthew 12:43-45).

The vinedresser also stated that he would fertilize the tree. This word "fertilize" was translated from the Greek phrase "ballo kopria." The King James version translates this as "dung it." This phrase means to violently throw and thrust dung. Did you ever feel like "ballo kopria" was taking place in your life? If we are honest, we will admit that many times we feel like "dung" is being thrown at us – and it is being thrown violently! What we must understand is that the purpose of the dung is fertilization; it is not to make our lives stink!

As a result of the vinedresser's work of digging and fertilizing, the tree produces fruit. Fruit is the outcome of a work being done not by the tree, but by the tree keeper!

> John 15:1-2 KJV I am the true vine, and My Father is the husbandman. Every branch in Me that beareth not fruit He taketh away: and every [branch] that beareth fruit, He purgeth it, that it may bring forth more fruit.

He is the vine and we are the branches. If a branch does not bear fruit it is "taken away." "Taken away" has also been translated as "cuts off," "cuts away," and "removes." What was Jesus articulating in this passage?

> Greek – AIRO: to *lift*; *take up*; figuratively to *raise*.
> To *expiate (make up for; do penance for)* sin: - away with sin, bear (up) sin, carry sin, lift up sin, loose sin, put away sin, remove sin, take (away, up) sin.

> Hebrew – NASA: *lift*, accept, advance, arise, (able to, [armor], suffer to) bear (-er, up), bring (forth), ease, forgive, furnish, further, give, go on, help, honorable (+ man), marry, magnify, pardon, raise (up), receive, regard, respect, set (up), spare.

Here we see two words that have similar definitions. These two words elucidate what Jesus was saying.

"NASA" and "AIRO" both involve being lifted up to a place pardon and forgiveness. Christ has paid the full price for our sin; He bore our sin and removed the penalty from us. He has more than made up for our sin; and in doing so, He removed our sin and guilt from us!

When we look at the Hebrew word "nasa" we find that its spelling paints a picture of the Holy Spirit connecting us to God and giving us the seed we need for life through the Word. It also shows us that we are shielded and supported by this life that Christ imparts through the Word and in turn we praise God for the fruit that is produced.

"Nasa" also represents ease. We must remember that that Word is our place of repose; it is our place of rest or ease. Ease represents being furnished with everything we need – the Word – and resting in that provision.

"Nasa" also means to marry; it means to connect yourself to Christ. When we are not bearing fruit we need to be reminded of who we are in Christ. It is imperative that we connect ourselves to Christ!

A branch that does not bear fruit is *not* taken away or taken out of the picture! This branch is lifted up; it is taken out of the dirt. Vines that are laying on the ground in the dirt are not producing fruit. If we are not bearing fruit we need lifted up – not beat down! We need to be taken out of the dirt – we need to get out of the flesh.

> 2 Corinthians 5:16-19 NKJV Therefore, from now on, we regard no one according to the flesh. Even though we have known Christ according to the flesh, yet now we know Him thus no longer. Therefore, if anyone is in Christ, he is a new creation; old things have passed away; behold, all things have become new. Now all things are of God, who has reconciled us to Himself through Jesus Christ, and has given us the ministry of reconciliation, that is, that God was in

Christ reconciling the world to Himself, not imputing their trespasses to them, and has committed to us the Word of reconciliation.

We are to no longer see ourselves, or others, based on the flesh. We are to see ourselves, and others, according to who we are in Christ! In Christ we *are* a *new* creation; a change *has* taken place through Christ. The "all things" that have become new are from God; their origin is in God through Christ – we have this new identity because of Christ; Jesus Christ has changed us! He has restored us; He has taken us back to our original intention.

God is not imputing our trespasses to us. God is not taking an inventory of our sin; He is not thinking on our sin – why are we? We have been given the Word of reconciliation – the Word of change through Christ, the Word of being restored to Divine favor.

Seeing the Word as a rule book instead of a love letter will keep us in this place of condemnation and keep us from producing Spiritual fruit. God gives us a choice – life or death. Do we want Spirit or flesh? Do we want to see ourselves according to the Spirit (life) or do we want to see ourselves according to the flesh (death)?

We need to be reminded of who we are in Christ if we are going to be productive Christians!

2 Peter 1:9 NIV But if anyone does not have them, he is nearsighted and blind, and has forgotten that he has been cleansed from his past sins.

After the list of what faith produces in your life is given, the Bible tells us that if we do not have these qualities in increasing measure it is because we do not know we are cleansed; we do not know the price has been completely paid for our sin. **If we do not understand who we are in Christ we will not bear fruit! Every branch that does not bring forth fruit the Father lifts up!** In Israel the vines are lifted up onto cross-shaped supports. What a beautiful picture of God's children being lifted up and abiding on the cross – resting on what Christ did for us so that we are able to produce fruit!

We are useless outside of Christ. Understanding this fact is fundamental in fruit production.

> John 15:6 NIV If anyone does not remain in Me, he is LIKE a branch that is thrown away and withers; such branches are picked up, thrown into the fire and burned.

If we are not abiding in Him and what He has accomplished for us we are *like* a branch that is useless. Those branches are burned up – just like the works we produce when we are not abiding in Christ! We can produce fruit that is no different from the fruit of an unsaved person when we are not resting in who we are in Christ.

A fruit-producing vine needs to be in its rightful place – it needs to be lifted up. We need to be lifted up, too; we need to take our place seated in Christ. A vine is not supposed to be in the dust. A vine that is crawling on the ground in the dust dies; it will not produce fruit! A Christian who lives in their sin or guilt will not produce fruit either.

> Psalms 18:23 AMP I was upright before Him and blameless with Him, ever [on guard] to keep myself free from my sin and guilt.

David kept himself free from his guilt and sin by abiding in the Word.

> Psalms 18:20-22 AMP   The Lord rewarded me according to my righteousness; according to the cleanness of my hands has He recompensed me. For I have kept the ways of the Lord and have not wickedly departed from my God. For all His ordinances were before me, and I put not away His statutes from me.

David *kept* the Word – he kept his focus on the Word; the Word was guarded in his life. The Word was before him – he kept his eyes on it.

David knew who he was in Christ. David understood that his righteousness was found in Christ and he knew the Lord treated him according to his righteousness – according to Jesus Christ!

We need to know who we are in Christ and we need to be focused on the Word if we are going to produce fruit. We need lifted out of the dirt – out of sin and guilt through Christ!

> Hebrews 9:14 NIV How much more, then, will the blood of Christ, who through the eternal Spirit offered Himself unblemished to God, cleanse our consciences from acts that lead to death, so that we may serve the living God!

Our consciences need to be cleansed – if not, all that we will accomplish will be works of the flesh – and the flesh is death. **The blood of Christ has purchased your clean conscience.** Whenever you are reminded of sin or guilt, you need to replace those thoughts with what the Word of God says regarding what Christ has done for you. Those thoughts that disagree with the Word of God should be your trigger to think thoughts that *do* line up with the Word.

If we are going to experience Spiritual growth we are going to have to know who we are in Christ! No matter what Spiritual fruit we desire in our lives, we must realize that it will only be produced when we are abiding in the Word and resting in what Christ has done for us.

CHAPTER 9

MATURE MATTERS

Ephesians 4:13 NIV
... until we all reach unity in the faith
and in the knowledge of the Son of God
and become mature, attaining to the
whole measure of the fullness of Christ.

Maturity. What is maturity and why do we need it? Maturity is completion and perfection according to the Bible. It is walking in the completion that Christ purchased for us. Our level of maturity is directly related to the amount of knowledge we have regarding God's Word. A mature Christian is personally acquainted with the Word. A mature Christian understands who they are in Christ; they recognize that they are lacking nothing *in Him*.

> Hebrews 5:13-14 NIV Anyone who lives on milk, being still an infant, is not acquainted with the teaching about righteousness. But solid food is for the mature, who by constant use have trained themselves to distinguish good from evil.

A mature Christian understands righteousness. They realize that Christ is their righteousness; they are not trying to earn or maintain a righteous standing. They find their worth and value in Him and in Him they are complete – lacking nothing!

A mature Christian is also continually digesting the Word of God. In the above verse from Hebrews, the word translated as "constant" means "because of." The word translated as "use" means "practice or habit." Because they are in the habit of taking in the Word of God, they know the difference between good and evil – between Spirit and flesh. The fourth chapter of Hebrews, verse twelve, also tells us that the Word of God divides between soul and Spirit.

The thoughts of a mature Christian line up with the Word of God. The more they abide in the Word, the more they think with the mind of Christ.

> 1 Corinthians 14:20 AMP Brethren, do not be children [immature] in your thinking; continue to be babes in [matters of] evil, but in your minds be mature [men].

Our thoughts are based on our intake of the Word. We must mature in our ways of thinking; we must fill ourselves with the Word.

Maturity is attained through the Word of God. Trials are one of the reasons we abide in the Word.

> James 1:2-3 NIV Consider it pure joy, my brothers, whenever you face trials of many kinds, because you know that the testing of your faith develops perseverance. Perseverance must finish its work so that you may be mature and complete, not lacking anything.

As we face conditions that contradict the Word of God, we must understand that our only weapon against these situations is the Word of God.

We are instructed to live by faith; faith is the substance of things unseen. Trials put our faith to the test. Is the Word true? Will we really see the promises of God come to pass in our lives? When our faith is tested we need to remain in the Word. It may seem hard to do this, but this is the only way we will conquer the trial and see the Word come to pass in our lives. As we abide in the Word, no matter what, we will begin to mature. The Word will enable us to grow; it provides us with everything we need to find our completeness in Christ. We take hold of this maturity through Christ alone.

> Colossians 1:28 MSG We preach Christ, warning people not to add to the Message. We teach in a spirit of profound common sense so that we can bring each person to maturity. To be mature is to be basic. Christ! No more, no less.

Too many times we try to add to what Christ has done. He has completed the work; it is finished! If we are going to mature, it is going to be because we are completely focused on Him!

We need to be mature if we are going to participate in ministry. Ephesians (chapter four and verses eleven through twelve) tells us that God has given us teachers and examples to aide in our development. These people have the gift of equipping the Saints with the Word; that is their ministry.

The Word completely furnishes us with everything we need to minister. Without the Word of God we will never mature; therefore, we will not be capable of ministry.

1 Timothy 3:6 NIV He must not be a recent convert, or he may become conceited and fall under the same judgment as the devil.

Recent converts are not to be put in ministry straight away. A new convert needs to mature. They need to be instructed in the Word and they need to abide in the Word on their own. A person who ministers must be grounded in the Word; they must be humble. **Humility is the foundation of ministering. If we begin to feel proud of what "we" do in ministry we must recognize that we are in the flesh. Ministry should leave us feeling grateful to God alone.**

Romans 15:13-14 YLT …the God of the hope shall fill you with all joy and peace in the believing, for your abounding in the hope in power of the Holy Spirit. And I am persuaded, my brethren--I myself also--concerning you, that ye yourselves also are full of goodness, having been filled with all knowledge, able also one another to admonish.

We become full of goodness and competent to instruct others *as* we believe in Him. We must never forget that faith only comes from taking in the Word of God. We are full of goodness because we are filled with all knowledge – filled with the Word of God. We are full and competent because of the Word we receive and cling to.

I am not able to help another Christian if I am immature – if I am not rooted in the Word. My intake of the Word equips me and matures me.

Ephesians 4:14-15 NIV Then we will no longer be infants, tossed back and forth by the waves, and blown here and there by every wind of teaching and by the cunning and craftiness of men in their deceitful scheming. Instead, speaking the truth in love, we will in all things grow up into Him who is the Head, that is, Christ.

As we take hold of the Word we begin to mature, and we will notice changes taking place. We will no longer be wavering back and forth; we will be sure of what we believe.

Our words begin to change as we mature. We will speak a new language of truth and love. We will find that our words are in agreement with God's; we will find that our words are rooted in His love for us.

We will not experience growth outside of truth. **The Word is essential for our growth.** The Word will lead us to experience all the fullness of Christ. The Word will enable us to take part in His nature rather than our flesh. Only when we are participating in His nature can we support and help another.

Ephesians 3:7-8 YLT …I became a ministrant, according to the gift of the grace of God that was given to me, according to the working of His power to me…

We cannot minister to another unless we are given the gift of grace and we have been given this gift! The gift of grace – the gift of His Divine influence in our daily lives – is the Word. We have been given the Word and it contains *everything* we need for life and for godliness.

Progressively abiding in the Word produces unmatched power. His power is made available to me through His Word. The Word produces faith and that faith produces miraculous fruit! We do not deserve any glory for the work of ministry (2 Corinthians 3:4-6).   The work of ministry is a Spiritual action; it must have a Spiritual source!

> 1 Timothy 1:12 KJV And I thank Christ Jesus our Lord, Who hath enabled me, for that He counted me faithful, putting me into the ministry.

> ENABLED: to empower. To strengthen and make strong.

> COUNTED: to lead; to command with authority.

Thankfulness comes when we understand where our strength comes from. It is Christ within us that gives us strength; we have no Spiritual strength on our own.

We see the phrase, "…He counted me faithful…" and this wording can lead us to assume something that is not true. We must look at the original text and define the original words that were translated into our English language. When we do this, we see that Jesus does not consider *us* faithful – He knows that He cannot trust in man (John 2:24). Instead, He "leads us faithfully."

> Jeremiah 32:38-40 NIV They will be My people, and I will be their God. I will give them singleness of heart and action, so that they will always fear Me for their own good and the good of their children after them. I will make an everlasting covenant with them: I will never stop doing good to them, and I will inspire them to fear Me, so that they will never turn away from Me.

Our God has gifted us with a heart that fears Him – and He did it for our own good! He leads us faithfully; He equips us with everything we need. He is not looking for us to possess some perfect qualities on our own. **We are used by God because *He* makes us usable!** A mature Christian views his ministry as a gift from God, he views it as empowered by God, and he views it as reason to praise God, not himself.

Our maturity will never be complete here in this realm. We must never feel as if we have "arrived." Pride can lead us to believe we have accomplished completeness, but humility will teach us differently.

> Philippians 3:12-14 NIV Not that I have already obtained all this, or have already been made perfect, but I press on to take hold of that for which Christ Jesus took hold of me. Brothers, I do not consider myself yet to have taken hold of it. But one thing I do: Forgetting what is behind and straining toward what is ahead, I press on toward the goal to win the prize for which God has called me heavenward in Christ Jesus.

Maturity is a process that will never be complete until we see Jesus face-to-face. At that time, He will change us in the twinkling of an eye (1 Corinthians 15:51-52). In understanding this, we must also understand that we can reach different levels of maturity here in this realm. We can press on to know Christ more and we can develop Spiritually.

Paul tells us that if we want to mature we must let go of the past. The past is the past; it is not my future! If I am going to move forward I must not turn back. This may be a strain, but it is worth the pain. When we allow our past to prevent our future we will not experience what God has for us. My husband once said, "Because of Christ, we are free to live today like yesterday never happened!"

Press on for the prize! What is the prize? The prize is that "heavenward calling" – it is maturing in Christ, becoming more and more like Him!

> 1 Corinthians 13:11 AMP When I was a child, I talked like a child, I thought like a child, I reasoned like a child; now that I have become a man, I am done with childish ways and have put them aside.

Childish ways are the ways of the flesh. The flesh will be put aside as we mature in the Word of God. As we abide in the Word our language will change, our thoughts will change, our motivation will change, and our actions will change.

> Romans 12:2 MSG Don't become so well-adjusted to your culture that you fit into it without even thinking. Instead, fix your attention on God. You'll be changed from the inside out...Unlike the culture around you, always dragging you down to its level of immaturity, God brings the best out of you, develops well-formed maturity in you.

As we fix our attention on God, we will change from the inside out. Too many are trying to change the outside without any interior transformation. **We will never notice lasting change without the Word of God; we must be fixed on the Word.** As we are focused on the Word, *God* will do the work in us that He has promised.

Maturity matters. It matters if we are ever going to take hold of all that Christ took hold of us for!

CHAPTER 10

MY TWO MINDS

Ephesians 4:17 NIV
So I tell you this, and insist on it in the Lord,
that you must no longer live as the Gentiles do,
in the futility of their thinking.

We understand that we have two natures and with these two natures comes two different methods of thinking. We have been given a new nature, a Spiritual nature, and part of this nature is the mind of Christ.

> 1 Corinthians 2:16 NIV "For who has known the mind of the Lord that He may instruct Him?" But we have the mind of Christ.

This word translated as "instruct" also means to unite with. How can we unite with God if we do not know how He thinks? We cannot; that is why we are given the mind of Christ. We have been given access to the thoughts of God through His Word. We can think in agreement with God because we abide in the Word and faith is produced.

> Proverbs 12:5 KJV The thoughts of the righteous [are] right: [but] the counsels of the wicked [are] deceit.

We must recognize that we now have a new nature and with that nature comes the ability to think righteous thoughts; thoughts that are in line with the Word of God. We must also make a decision regarding this ability. What are we going to do with this ability? Are we going to abide in the Word and take hold of it or are we going to ignore it and go on thinking in the futility of our flesh? **The thoughts of the Spirit *will be* righteous; but, the thoughts of the flesh *will be* deceitful.**

The unsaved have useless thoughts. Their ideas contradict the Word and they mean nothing.

> Psalms 10:4 AMP The wicked one in the pride of his countenance will not seek, inquire for, and yearn for God; all his thoughts are that there is no God [so He never punishes].

The flesh does not even acknowledge God. The thoughts of the flesh do not acknowledge Him, either. The flesh ignores the Word of God and the flesh is proud of this. The flesh does not believe that there is a price to pay for sin; the flesh does not believe that Christ paid that price for us. The thoughts of the flesh are futile; they lead men away from Jesus Christ.

> Psalms 94:11 AMP The Lord knows the thoughts of man, that they are vain (empty and futile--only a breath).

We can have thoughts like these, too, if we are focused on the flesh. On the other hand; if we concentrate on the Word, we can produce thoughts with Spiritual value.

Thoughts of the flesh will fight for the right to occupy your mind, but you can win this fight with the Word. David experienced this fight. Many of the Psalms display this fight. Psalms, chapter thirty-one, is one such Psalm. David speaks of the trials in his life and he describes his pain, but in verse fourteen something changes.

> Psalms 31:14-16 NIV But I trust in You, O LORD; I say, "You are my God." My times are in Your hands; deliver me from my enemies and from those who pursue me. Let Your face shine on Your servant; save me in Your unfailing love.

David interjects with a "but." No matter what was going on in his life, David knew that he could trust in God. Many were coming against him, *but* God was his Deliverer. The wrong thoughts were occupying David's mind and they were coming out of his mouth; but praise be to God, he knew how to turn things around.

> Psalms 94:19 AMP In the multitude of my [anxious] thoughts within me, Your comforts cheer and delight my soul!

David knew where to go for what he needed! David went to the Word and the Word changed his thoughts. The Word comforted him and it brought him joy – the thoughts of the flesh sure did not!

He began to speak the Word. He declared what was true, or what was Spiritual, in place of his feelings of the flesh. David understood that the thoughts of the flesh were lies. As we abide in the Word we will begin to recognize which thoughts are ineffectual lies and which thoughts are Spiritual truth.

David may have said some futile words in the heat of the moment, but he did not stop there. He spoke words of life to destroy those words of death. We need to do the same. The wrong thoughts will come against us during times of trial; we must know how to get rid of them.

> 2 Corinthians 10:5 AMP [Inasmuch as we] refute arguments and theories and reasonings and every proud and lofty thing that sets itself up against the [true] knowledge of God; and we lead every thought and purpose away captive into the obedience of Christ (the Messiah, the Anointed One).

We do not have to believe anything that disagrees with the Word of God. In Christ we have the power to make our thoughts line up with His. We can make thoughts obedient to Christ *by knowing the Word of God.* When we begin to think anything that does not agree with the Word we will recognize it and we will know the Word well enough to replace that wrong thought with a Spiritual thought in the same way David did!

We must be completely convinced that a mind that thinks the thoughts of the flesh is Spiritually useless if we are going to find this fight worth fighting.

> Romans 8:5-8 KJV For they that are after the flesh do mind the things of the flesh; but they that are after the Spirit the things of the Spirit. For to be carnally minded [is] death; but to be spiritually minded [is] life and peace. Because the carnal mind [is] enmity against God: for it is not subject to the law of God, neither indeed can be. So then they that are in the flesh cannot please God.

Our thoughts are very significant. Our carnal thoughts are destructive. We can give our minds over to the flesh if we believe that such thoughts are harmless. Anything that our flesh is in agreement with is hatred toward God and it *is* Spiritually devastating to us.

> Proverbs 23:7a AMP For as he thinks in his heart, so is he.

Our thoughts determine our characteristics and our actions. If we continually think according to the flesh, we will be controlled by our flesh and we will produce the fruit of the flesh. This is Spiritually devastating!

> Jeremiah 17:10 NIV "I the LORD search the heart and examine the mind, to reward a man according to his conduct, according to what his deeds deserve."

The Lord examines the mind. The King James Version says that "the Lord...tries the reins." The Hebrew word for "mind" is also the Hebrew word for "reins." This is very interesting. What is a rein? A rein is any means of restraint or of control. Do we understand the power our minds have? I do not believe that we do. If we did, we would not allow our minds the power to wander excessively. We would fill ourselves with the Word if we truly believed that our minds determined our outcome.

The Lord examines or tests our thoughts. As a man thinks, so is he – if he thinks Spiritually, he is walking in his Spiritual identity. If his thoughts are those of the flesh, he is walking in his carnal identity. The Spiritual mind is in agreement with the Word; the Spiritual mind is focused on the Word and because of this faith is produced – the only thing that pleases God. This faith then produces the fruit of the Spirit in our lives. Our Spiritual thoughts produce the Spiritual fruit that every Christian should be producing. If I think according to the Word of God, I will become what the Word of God proclaims.

Our conduct cannot be tested by appearance. Many times we can produce fruit that *looks* Spiritual, but if we could take a look inside we would see something that is not in agreement with the Word of God. God looks at the inside; God determines the worth of our actions by their source. The actions that originate in the Spirit will be rewarded and we will place those crowns at the feet of Jesus – He is the Source; He is the reason those actions were produced.

It is time for us to take an inventory of our thoughts. We need to think about what we are thinking about. We need to take the thoughts that disagree with the Word of God and we need to make them agree with the Word by filling our minds with that Word.

> Isaiah 55:7 NIV Let the wicked forsake his way and the evil man his thoughts. Let him turn to the LORD, and He will have mercy on him, and to our God, for He will freely pardon.

> Hebrews 3:1 NIV Therefore, holy brothers, who share in the heavenly calling, fix your thoughts on Jesus, the apostle and high priest whom we confess.

Through Christ we can change our thoughts; we have the power in Christ to control what we are thinking. The Word of God is our weapon against the thoughts of the flesh.

It is time for us to recognize the fruit that a mind that is in agreement with the flesh produces.

Psalms 55:2 NIV …My thoughts trouble me and I am distraught.

The thoughts of the flesh trouble us; they do not do anything of value for us. These thoughts steal time from us. These thoughts leave us living a life that is unfruitful Spiritually.

We have been given the gift of a new nature and we can now think in agreement with God.

Colossians 3:1-3 KJV If ye then be risen with Christ, seek those things which are above, where Christ sitteth on the right hand of God. Set your affection on things above, not on things on the earth. For ye are dead, and your life is hid with Christ in God.

We are now risen with Christ; because of this, we can seek the Spiritual things that Christ has accomplished for us. We can go after all that Christ has for us by setting our affection on Spiritual things. "Setting our affections" means to exercise our mind or be of the same mind as Christ. The more we remain in the Word, the more our minds take on our new identity.

Everything about our flesh is death. The flesh is unquestionably futile. That is why Jesus Christ defeated our flesh for us. See yourself in Christ. Get in agreement with what Christ has done for you. Renew your mind by taking in the Word of God.

Ephesians 4:22-24 AMP Strip yourselves of your former nature [put off and discard your old unrenewed self] which characterized your previous manner of life and becomes corrupt through lusts and desires that spring from delusion; And be constantly renewed in the spirit of your mind [having a fresh mental and spiritual attitude], And put on the new nature (the regenerate self) created in God's image, [Godlike] in true righteousness and holiness.

We have the ability in Christ to "put off" the old nature. This means that we can lay the flesh aside and walk in our new nature. The flesh will take a back seat *if* we will abide in the Word. As we abide in the Word we are "putting on" the new nature. We are covering ourselves with who God says we are and what God says we can do. We are truly holy and righteous in Christ; we do not have to live a life of lust, evil desire, and delusion. We can know the truth and we can be set free from the power the flesh has over our mind. This is a constant process, however.

John 8:31-32 KJV   Then said Jesus to those Jews which believed on Him, If ye continue in My word, [then] are ye My disciples indeed; And ye shall know the truth, and the truth shall make you free.

If we continue in the Word, then we are a disciple or a student of the Word; and then, we will know the truth and we will be set free. A disciple is not a person who hears the Word once or twice; they are studying the Word and they are Spiritually knowledgeable.   Many times we hear our freedom being declared without mentioning the process by which that freedom comes. **Being set free is the *result* of continuing in the Word! If we do not *continue* in the Word of God, we will not be full of truth; subsequently, we will not experience freedom.**
Our minds need to be set free! Our minds need to be full of the Word! For many years our minds have been set on

the things of the flesh. For many years we did not know any better; however, we now know how to renew our minds and think with the mind of Christ.

Our flesh cannot understand anything Spiritual. I am thankful for the new nature I was given; because of what Christ has done for me, I can now think like the new creation I am!

CHAPTER 11

LIVE LIKE

Colossians 2:6-7 NIV
So then, just as you received Christ Jesus as Lord,
continue to live in Him, rooted and built up in Him,
strengthened in the faith as you were taught,
and overflowing with thankfulness.

We are told to live in the same way we received Christ. What does that mean? How did we receive Christ?

> Ephesians 2:8-9 NIV For it is by grace you have been saved, through faith--and this not from yourselves, it is the gift of God-- not by works, so that no one can boast.

Our lives must be lived by grace through faith. Again, the Greek word that "grace" is translated from means: the Divine influence on our heart in our daily lives. This Divine influence is the Word of God. The Word is what changes us; it is our Spiritual inspiration and power and it must be regarded daily. We are to live in the Word day after day; as we do, faith is being produced (Romans 10:17). **We are living "by grace through faith" when we persist in the Word of God.**

A life that is lived by grace through faith will be a life void of boasting. We understand that apart from Christ we can do nothing of Spiritual value; so, we give Him all the honor and glory.

In living "by grace through faith," we repeatedly see the thankfulness aspect. Living life in the same way we received Christ makes us thankful because we understand it is all about Christ and it is not because of us. **We cannot *produce* what we need; we can only *receive* it. Receivers are thankful; they understand appreciation.**

> Colossians 3:17 KJV And whatsoever ye do in word or deed, [do] all in the name of the Lord Jesus, giving thanks to God and the Father by Him.

The humble live a life that is superior to the rest! They are living a life that is full of Spiritual fruit. They are doing whatever they do through Christ and they know that He deserves all of the honor and the glory.

> Colossians 1:12-13 AMP Giving thanks to the Father, Who has qualified and made us fit to share the portion which is the inheritance of the saints (God's holy people) in the Light. [The Father] has delivered and drawn us to Himself out of the control and the dominion of darkness and has transferred us into the kingdom of the Son of His love.

God qualified us; we did not make ourselves eligible. God made us fit; we did not make ourselves capable. We have so much to be thankful for! The person who believes that they make themselves eligible by works is not appreciative and they live unthankful lives. They will instead be expecting God to show them His thankfulness.

The Father delivers us, the Father draws us to Him – the Father is responsible for our deliverance and our life in the Spirit.   He gives us the ability to "imitate" Him; because of what He has done for us, we can live a life that is reproducing Christ in this world.

> Ephesians 5:1-5 KJV   Be ye therefore followers of God, as dear children;   And walk in love, as Christ also hath loved us, and hath given Himself for us an offering and a sacrifice to God for a sweetsmelling savour.   But fornication, and all uncleanness, or covetousness, let it not be once named among you, as becometh saints;   Neither filthiness, nor foolish talking, nor jesting, which are not convenient: but rather giving of thanks.   For this ye know, that no whoremonger, nor unclean person, nor covetous man, who is an idolater, hath any inheritance in the kingdom of Christ and of God.

A follower is an imitator.   A follower of God emulates the life of God.   The fruit of the flesh is not "convenient" for a follower of God – it is not correct.   A follower of God *will* produce Spiritual fruit.

What should be named among us or what should we as Christians be known for when we live as imitators of God? Thankfulness! We should be known for giving God thanks. When we are thankful we are participating in the Spiritual nature; we are emulating God. Christ is being reproduced in me as I abide in the Word and that will lead to being thankful; it is correct for the follower of God to be thankful.

When we are imitating God we are also seeking the kingdom of God – we are living the life of a dearly loved child of God and we are experiencing what God has to offer. Love is the foundation for thankfulness. If we recognize the love of God that is in Christ Jesus, thankfulness will be a given. Christ was offered on our behalf; He is our sacrifice. Because of what He has done for us, we are seen as saints; no longer do we have to be recognized as unclean.

We see a list of various sins that are the obvious fruit of the person who is not a follower of God, but we must understand that being unthankful is sin, also. The sin of being unthankful might not be as easily recognized, but it is death just the same – it will not produce anything of value in our lives. We are participating in idolatry when we believe that we deserve thanks *from* God. We are placing ourselves in the place that belongs to God.

We could never deliver ourselves from the dominion of darkness. What makes man think that he can? What made the Israelites decide that they wanted to perform instead of receiving the Word? I believe it is simply pride. Pride keeps man from receiving. Pride demands earning and pride therefore desires recognition.

> Psalms 119:21 KJV Thou hast rebuked the proud [that are] cursed, which do err from Thy commandments.

Pride is a curse. Pride is contrary to the truth of the Word of God. The arrogant "err" from God's Word –they stray from it. The Hebrew word for the proud is spelled with two Hebrew letters. Each letter in the Hebrew alphabet represent something. The two letters that spell "proud" represent a closed tent door and the sword or the Word. The proud are closed off from the Word.

Many times Satan interjects that we are weak when we are dependent, but that is a lie. We must know the truth.

Psalms 119:69 KJV   The proud have forged a lie
against me: [but] I will keep Thy precepts with [my]
whole heart.

When we know the truth we will not fall for the lie.
Remaining focused on the Word and protecting the Word in
your life will make you familiar with truth.   In the garden,
Satan worked on man's pride. He told man that he could be
like God without any help from God.   Being like God is
something that *is* available to us – God wants us to be
imitators of Him! Satan took this simple truth and distorted it
by adding his lie.   Satan told man that if he just did one
simple act on his own, he could be like God. He told man
that the work of his hands could result in living like God.
Again we see mixture. What a destructive force mixture is!
No matter what we can accomplish on our own, it will never
exceed what God has to offer us as a gift.

Proverbs 16:19 KJV Better [it is to be] of an humble
spirit with the lowly, than to divide the spoil with the
proud.

We can divide the spoil with the proud – we can take
part in taking account of what we can accomplish on our
own, but it will never be beneficial to us. It is better to be
humble and receive from Christ. It is better to understand
that He is our everything and that apart from Him we can do
nothing. We must find our life in Christ.

Are you rooted and built up in Him? Roots are very
important. They are necessary for life. Roots absorb and
store the required water, food, and nutrients; they serve as an
anchor; they determine growth.

Are you rooted in Christ? Do you absorb the Word and store it up?

> Jeremiah 17:8 KJV For he shall be as a tree planted by the waters, and [that] spreadeth out her roots by the river, and shall not see when heat cometh, but her leaf shall be green; and shall not be careful in the year of drought, neither shall cease from yielding fruit.

Are you living a life that is rooted in the Word? The planting that can withstand the heat has roots in the water. Where are your roots? The Word is referred to as water many times in the Scripture; are your roots in the Water?

> Psalms 1:2-3 KJV …his delight [is] in the law of the LORD; and in His law doth he meditate day and night. And he shall be like a tree planted by the rivers of water, that bringeth forth his fruit in his season; his leaf also shall not wither; and whatsoever he doeth shall prosper.

Are you living like this tree that is planted by the water? Are you living a life that delights in the Word of God?

Many times people ask me for advice. I hope I never get to the point where I offer my ideas over the Word of God. There are times when people do not want to hear the Word of God, but I give it nevertheless. **Nothing can rectify our problems like the Word of God. When the heat comes, we need the Word! We do not need pity, we do not need man's ideas, we do not need to run away – we need the Word!**

The longest branch that you see on the tree is indicative of the longest root you do not see. The Word that we store up inside of us will be revealed in our lives one day. We need to be rooted in Christ if we want to experience a life that will declare Christ to the world.

Are you rooted in Christ? Are you anchored in Christ?

> Hebrews 6:17-20 NIV Because God wanted to make the unchanging nature of His purpose very clear to the heirs of what was promised, He confirmed it with an oath. God did this so that, by two unchangeable things in which it is impossible for God to lie, we who have fled to take hold of the hope offered to us may be greatly encouraged. We have this hope as an anchor for the soul, firm and secure. It enters the inner sanctuary behind the curtain, where Jesus, who went before us, has entered on our behalf...

We have an anchor; we have the Word of God. God gave us His promises and His promises are all truth. We never have to wonder if God will keep His Word; it is impossible for Him to lie.

For us to be anchored in Christ we must be anchored in the Word. The Word must be our priority.

> Galatians 3:3 NIV Are you so foolish? After beginning with the Spirit, are you now trying to attain your goal by human effort? Have you suffered so much for nothing...

Human effort will never produce Spiritual fruit. We must be convinced that the Word of God is our single Spiritual source. We can become easily confused if we do not hold on to the truth.

Paul suggests that it is foolish to try to live by human effort. Part of the definition of foolish is sensual. Works appeal to our carnal nature. Our effort appeals to our mind, too. Who would think that doing something "good" could be wrong? Our carnal minds hit the proverbial wall when we consider this. We have lived lives that encourage working to earn. If you study enough you will get a good grade, if you work hard enough you will be paid well, and so on. Everything that we have been taught agrees with human effort, but when does God ever agree with man?

Romans 3:4a NIV Not at all! Let God be true, and every man a liar.

No matter what we may think, if it does not line up with the Word of God it is not true. God has given us His prescription for life and it is to abide in the Word of God. No matter how many other ideas man may have, they will all continue to be wrong. Only living a life in the Word will produce the Spiritual lifestyle God longs for us to have.

How are you living? Are you living a Spiritual life? If you are continuing in Christ, rooted and built up in Him, and strengthened in your faith, then you will be living like the Spiritual creation you are!

CHAPTER 12

MR. "DO RIGHT"

2 Kings 14:3 KJV
And he did [that which was] right in the sight of
the LORD, yet not like David his father:
he did according to all things as Joash his father did.
Howbeit the high places were not taken away:
as yet the people did sacrifice and burnt
incense on the high places.

Amaziah had been influenced by his father Joash. Amaziah did things the way his father did things, not the way King David did. What is the difference between the way David lived his life and the way Joash did? Let's find out.

David relied on God to work through Him. David's name comes from the Hebrew word "dod." This word means: lover, a love token, friend. David had a relationship with God – he was not in relationship with rules and regulations. David accomplished Spiritual actions because he kept his focus on the Lord.

Amaziah did what was "right" to *the eye*. If you looked at what he was doing it would look Spiritual, but a closer look will reveal that it was not. Previously, when we looked at the third chapter of Revelation, we found that our works are not what God requires – no matter how "good" they give the impression of being.

God is not impressed by how Spiritual our actions look. We need to stop being concerned with how things appear.

> John 7:24 NIV   Stop judging by mere appearances, and make a right judgment.

We can judge a book by its cover, but we cannot always judge a book by its cover *appropriately*. Amaziah, to the eye, did what the law said to do, but that was not enough. The Word says, "howbeit the high places…" Howbeit means "yet." This means that even though things looked good on the outside, Amaziah's works were not Spiritual. He could not fulfill what the law required.

It is vital for us to understand that the flesh cannot produce anything Spiritual and the flesh cannot destroy something carnal.

Amaziah did what looked good, but he was not like David. David was a man after God's own heart.

> 1 Samuel 13:14 YLT   And, now, thy kingdom doth not stand, Jehovah hath sought for Himself a man ACCORDING TO HIS OWN HEART, and Jehovah chargeth him for leader over His people, for thou hast not KEPT that which Jehovah commanded thee.

David was a man according to God's own heart. This word for man is not the same word used when God said He created "man." This word describes a champion; it portrays a conqueror; it is not simply referring to a human being.

The Hebrew spelling for this word translated as man shows us that humility is the center of being a champion, a steward (someone in charge of something that does not belong to them). A "man" will connect with God and be an indication of Him when he understands who he really is. True humility understands our importance and value are only found in Christ. True humility will make you Christ-like!

ACCORDING TO: in agreement with. Render somebody something. To bestow something such as a blessing on somebody.

David was in agreement with who God said he was. He received from the Lord and he reigned. David saw himself the way God saw him – David walked by grace through faith. David "kept" the Word; David's focus was on the Word and he received from God.

Psalms 119:11 KJV Thy Word have I hid in mine heart, that I might not sin *against Thee.*

David hid the Word in his heart; the word "hid" means to hoard; to protect; to esteem. David kept his eyes on the Word. He hedged the Word in; he protected the Word; he stored the Word up inside of him. He admired the Word and had high regard for it – this was evident in his actions.

David understood that the Word kept him from sin. As we look at this part of the verse we must take note that the phrase "against Thee" was added to the text; this phrase is not in the original Hebrew text. We are not doing something *to* God when we sin. We are walking in the nature that disagrees with the Word; however, and our actions will be of the flesh – they will be sin. We should not feel like we are doing something *to* God when we sin. We must realize that we sin because we are in the flesh and we should then quickly get the focus back to the Word of God. God left us with this nature of the flesh; He did not leave us with it so that we could sin against Him or do something hurtful to Him. He left us with the flesh in hopes that our flesh would draw us closer to Him (Romans 8:20-21). When we feel like we are doing something "against God" this leads to staying away from God, not drawing close to Him.

We also find that David was in agreement with God's Covenant, not man's.

> 2 Chronicles 6:14 NIV He said: "O LORD, God of Israel, there is no God like You in heaven or on earth--You who keep Your covenant of love with Your servants who continue wholeheartedly in Your way."

> 2 Chronicles 6:16 NIV   Now LORD, God of Israel, keep for Your servant David my father the promises You made to him when You said, You shall never fail to have a man to sit before Me on the throne of Israel, if only your sons are careful in all they do to walk before Me according to My law, as you have done.

David accomplished things God's way, not man's; the two are very different. God's covenant was founded on love; man's covenant was founded on compulsory works. We have to choose which one we will follow. Will we walk in His Spirit or will we walk in our flesh; the choice is ours to make.

> Exodus 19:5 KJV Now therefore, if ye will obey My voice indeed, and keep My covenant, then ye shall be a peculiar treasure unto Me above all people: for all the earth [is] Mine:

> Exodus 19:8 KJV   And all the people answered together, and said, All that the LORD hath spoken we

will do. And Moses returned the words of the people unto the LORD.

Bear in mind that God's plan was for us to "shama" and "shamar" the Word while man's plan was to "asah" the Word. We recall that man audaciously proclaimed that he would *accomplish* everything God had spoken only to find himself worshipping a golden calf shortly after this declaration of performance. **Man's plan to execute the Word is diametrically opposed to God's plan of absolute dependence on the Word.** The manumission of man will never be accomplished by works of the flesh; only Christ can set us free from sin.

David knew that he needed the Word; because of this, David walked in the Word. This means that he spent time in the Word, walking to and fro, treading all about.

> Psalms 119:45 AMP And I will walk at liberty and at ease, for I have sought and inquired for [and desperately required] Your precepts.

David spent a lot of time in the Word. He experienced freedom and ease because he sought the Word in his life!

> SOUGHT: to *tread* or *frequent*; usually to *follow* (for pursuit or search); to *seek* or *ask*; specifically to *worship:* - care for, diligently, require, search, seek [for, out], surely.

"To seek" means "to worship;" when you recall the definition of worship (from chapter 4) you realize that David was cared for by God, he was supported by God, he was aided by God, God assisted him, and God nurtured him.

David was dependent on God; he required the Word in his life; thus, it was demonstrated in his life.

> Psalms 119:14-16 KJV I have rejoiced in the way of Thy testimonies, as [much as] in all riches. I will meditate in Thy precepts, and have respect unto Thy ways. I will delight myself in Thy statutes: I will not forget Thy word.

> Psalms 119:20 KJV My soul breaketh for the longing [that it hath] unto Thy judgments at all times.

David realized the value of the Word; he was desperate for it. He esteemed it above all. David rejoiced in the Word; the Word gave him joy. The Word was on David's mind; he meditated on the Word because he understood its worth.

> Psalms 27:4 KJV One [thing] have I desired of the LORD, that will I seek after; that I may dwell in the house of the LORD all the days of my life, to behold the beauty of the LORD, and to enquire in His temple.

David's priority was the Word; Amaziah's was not! David knew that the Word was his life so he knew that he needed to keep his attention focused on it; it was the *one* thing he required. This resulted in the Spiritual actions we read about in the Word when we read about David's life.

When we look at David's life we also notice that he walked in the flesh at different times, in the same way everyone does. As we study these times of walking in the flesh we discover what leads us down that path.

2 Samuel 12:9 KJV Wherefore hast thou despised the commandment of the LORD, to do evil in His sight? thou hast killed Uriah the Hittite with the sword, and hast taken his wife [to be] thy wife, and hast slain him with the sword of the children of Ammon.

Nathan came to David after he had Uriah the Hittite put to death; he confronted him about this situation. Nathan revealed why David found himself in the flesh: it was because he "despised" the Word of God. The Hebrew word that was translated as despised means to disesteem and disdain. David found himself in a temporary situation where he no longer respected or valued the Word of God in the way he used to. This lack of value that he assigned to the Word brought him face-to-face with his flesh and the death that it produces.

When we do not appreciate the true significance of the Word we will wander away from the Word. **The Word is not a priority to the person who regards it as anything less than their very life.** When we ignore the Word we will find ourselves in the flesh and the flesh will only produce works of the flesh.

If we are going to enjoy the fruit of the Spirit we are going to have to make the Word our priority. It is going to be the *one* thing we desire; the *one* thing we look to for Spiritual fruit.

For whatever reason, David was no longer depending on *one* thing. The Word was not his focus and he found himself in sin. We will experience the same when we disregard the Word. The Bible specifically declares that anything that is not of faith is sin (Romans 14:23). Faith is the result of hearing the Word; therefore, a lack of the Word leaves us with the fruit of our flesh. **Sin is the direct result of ignoring the Word of God.**

> 2 Corinthians 9:8 NIV And God is able to make all grace abound to you, so that in all things at all times, having all that you need, you will abound in every good work.

> Deuteronomy 30:11-14 NIV Now what I am commanding you today is not too difficult for you or beyond your reach. It is not up in heaven, so that you have to ask, "Who will ascend into heaven to get it and proclaim it to us so we may obey it?" Nor is it beyond the sea, so that you have to ask, "Who will cross the sea to get it and proclaim it to us so we may obey it?" NO, THE WORD IS VERY NEAR YOU; IT IS IN YOUR MOUTH AND IN YOUR HEART SO YOU MAY OBEY IT.

God has made all grace abound to us by presenting us with the gift of His Word. If we want to thrive with Spiritual fruit we must first have the Word in our heart and our mouth. We must incessantly store up the Word if we are ever going to produce a Spiritual harvest.

God did not give us rules to live up to. God gave us His Word; He gave us the ability to live like He lives. If we are going to do "right," we must understand what the Word is to us.

CHAPTER 13

CONFIDENT CHRISTIAN

Hebrews 3:14 KJV
For we are made partakers of Christ,
if we hold the beginning of our
confidence steadfast unto the end.

We need confidence. We need to be certain that Christ is all that we need. If we want to be a partaker of Christ, or a person who shares in His nature, we must be confident.

The beginning of our confidence is the chief part of our confidence. How did we begin our Spiritual journey? We began by receiving what Christ did for us by faith. The beginning of our confidence is Christ alone. We will make it to the "end," or the completion of the process that is taking place in us, when we are confident in Christ alone. The end does not refer to the end of life in this realm. It simply refers to the time when you experience what the Word will do in your life. As we abide in the Word of God our lives begin to change. We begin to progressively participate in the nature of Christ.

> Hebrews 3:12-19 KJV Take heed, brethren, lest there be in any of you an evil heart of unbelief, in departing from the living God...For we are made partakers of Christ, if we hold the beginning of our confidence steadfast unto the end; While it is said, Today if ye will hear His voice, harden not your hearts, as in the

provocation. For some, when they had heard, did provoke: howbeit not all that came out of Egypt by Moses. But with whom was He grieved forty years? [was it] not with them that had sinned, whose carcases fell in the wilderness? And to whom sware He that they should not enter into His rest, but to them that believed not? So we see that they could not enter in because of unbelief.

We cannot participate in the Divine nature if we are not abiding in the Word of God. When God instructed man to live by the Word they decided to live by works; this is referred to here as the provocation. **They provoked the Lord by choosing death over life, by choosing their works over His.** If you read the entire third chapter of Hebrews, then you will see that God was not in favor of man's decision to perform the Word instead of living in the Word. God said that they did not know His ways; they did not know the covenant of the faith. They did not know that the Word of God was meant to be their life. They had no confidence in what God said the Word would do for them.

When we refuse to see the Word as our life we will live a life of unrest. True rest is only found in Christ – we cannot enter His rest when we are not living by faith. We know that faith comes from hearing the Word, so we also know that rest is not possible outside of the Word. They could not enter His rest because they viewed the Word as something they could live up to. Their confidence was in themselves. We cannot find true confidence outside of Christ.

Proverbs 1:22 AMP How long, O simple ones [open to evil], will you love being simple? And the scoffers delight in scoffing and [self-confident] fools hate knowledge?

God refers to those who are self-confident as simple and foolish. The "simple" refers to being open to evil or yielding to the flesh. Our flesh encourages us to find confidence in ourselves, but the Spirit teaches us otherwise.

> Proverbs 3:5 AMP Lean on, trust in, and be confident in the Lord with all your heart and mind and do not rely on your own insight or understanding.

Our confidence is to be properly placed in Christ alone. Relying on ourselves is detrimental. We cannot depend on ourselves; we still have a flesh to deal with and it is extremely unreliable.

> Jeremiah 17:5 NIV This is what the LORD says: "Cursed is the one who trusts in man, who depends on flesh for his strength and whose heart turns away from the LORD."

When we depend on man, or ourselves, God says that we are cursed. What does it mean to be cursed?

> Deuteronomy 28:15 KJV But it shall come to pass, if thou wilt not hearken unto the voice of the LORD thy God, to observe to do all His commandments and His statutes which I command thee this day; that all these curses shall come upon thee, and overtake thee:

Deuteronomy, chapter twenty-eight, lists what it means to be cursed in verses fifteen through sixty-eight. At the beginning of Deuteronomy we see the blessings and we see how to walk in those blessings.

The blessings include a blessed family life, a blessed occupation, victory over the enemy, success, and joy, just to name a few. After the blessings are listed, God again reminds us of the key to living this life.

> Deuteronomy 28:14 NIV Do not turn aside from any of the commands I give you today, to the right or to the left, following other gods and serving them.

These blessings would be realized only if they would keep their focus on the Word of God. He gave them living oracles – He gave them the prescription for life as He has it. They simply needed to place their confidence in Him and remain focused on the Word.

They were told to "hearken" to the voice of the Lord. "Hearken" was translated from the Hebrew word "shama." We recall that the word "shama" meant to hear intelligently, to be attentive; to agree with. It also meant to be content with, to understand, and to be able to tell others about.

They were also told to "observe" His commandments. This is translated from the Hebrew word "shamar." We recall that this means to hedge in, to remain focused on, and to protect.

The blessings and the curses are the result of whether or not we "shama" and "shamar" the Word of God. When we are depending upon ourselves we are not attending to the Word; we are focused on ourselves and we are cursed. Trusting in man will never bring us into the blessings of God.

Confidence that is placed in Christ leads us to depend on the Word instead of ourselves. As we place our confidence in Christ, we begin to abide in the Word of God more and more. We "shama" and we "shamar" and we walk in the blessings.

We must never forget that we cannot put confidence in ourselves or anything we can accomplish apart from Christ. Partake of all that Christ has purchased for you with His blood – keep your confidence properly placed in Him!

CHAPTER 14

VICTORY OVER THE FLESH

1 John 5:4 NKJV
For whatever is born of God overcomes the world.
And this is the victory that has overcome
the world--our faith.

Whatever is born of God overcomes the world. What is born of God? Your new nature, your Spiritual nature, is born of God. When you received Christ's sacrifice for your sins the Bible declares that you were "born again." This was a birth of Spirit. When you were born in the natural, it was a birth of water.

> John 3:5 NIV Jesus answered, "I tell you the truth, no one can enter the kingdom of God unless he is born of water *and* the Spirit."

We enter the Spiritual realm when we receive Christ and the work that He completed for us. We are now born of God; and according to the Scripture, we can now overcome the world.

How did we receive this new birth? We received it by faith. Faith is our victory.

We have been saved from sin's penalty by grace through faith. We must continue to bear in mind that grace is translated from a word that means "the Divine influence upon the heart reflected in our daily life" and that God's daily influence in your life comes from His Word. The Word is the foundation on which we receive Christ. Without the Word there can be no faith; we need to hear the words of God in order to experience this new birth. We cannot lead someone to Christ without the Word.

> Ephesians 1:13 NIV And you also were included in Christ when you heard the Word of truth, the gospel of your salvation. Having believed, you were marked in him with a seal, the promised Holy Spirit.

We take on the new nature, we are included in Christ, when we receive what Christ has accomplished for us. We hear the Word, faith is produced, and we are given a new identity. A new life in Christ is now ours.

We understand that we receive this new birth by faith and we are also aware that the Word tells us that we are to live in the same way that we received Christ (Colossians 2:6).

We are to live by grace through faith. We are to remain in the Word; and when we do so, we live out the influence it has on us. As a result of doing this, we will find ourselves walking in victory.

The Word is the victory that overcomes the world; it is the victory that overcomes our flesh.

> Romans 12:21 NIV Do not be overcome by evil, but overcome evil with good.

We cannot prevail over the flesh with our flesh. Our flesh is inherently evil; it is not "of God." Our Spirit, however, is born of God; it is good. We have the power within us when we are born again; we can overcome the flesh because of the Holy Spirit of God that dwells in us.

There may be two parts to each of us, but the flesh does not have to be the part that rules over us. If we choose to live by grace – by God's Divine influence in our daily lives – we will live a life where sin no longer reigns.

> Romans 6:14-16 KJV   For sin shall not have dominion over you: for ye are not under the law, but under grace. What then? shall we sin, because we are not under the law, but under grace? God forbid. Know ye not, that to whom ye yield yourselves servants to obey, his servants ye are to whom ye obey; whether of sin unto death, or of obedience unto righteousness?

We find that sin cannot rule over us when we are abiding in the Word of God. If I am "under grace," I am living a life that is dependent on Christ (and He is the Word). When I am living by grace I will not be living a life controlled by sin. Some believe that grace is a "license to sin." These people clearly do not understand grace. God has forbid sin to have authority in the lives of those who live by grace. When the question, "Shall we sin under grace?" was posed, God's answer was, "God forbid." This phrase comes from two words, each of which mean: God forbid, God forbid. **God does not *allow* sin to reign in a Spiritual environment; He forbade this. He has ordered sin to take its rightful place – in the flesh. Sin only has dominion over us when we choose to live under the law.**

> 1 John 2:29 NIV If you know that He is righteous, you know that everyone who does what is right has been born of Him.

In order for us to be able to do what is "right," or more correctly – Spiritual, we must be born of God.

When we are doing what is right we know that we are participating in our Spiritual nature. Sin is at home in the flesh; Spiritual actions are at home in the Spirit. We are walking in the Spirit and producing Spiritual fruit because we understand that we have been born of Him – we understand that we have been born again; we now have a new Spiritual nature.

Those who are living a life that is influenced by the Word will not be controlled by sin.

> 1 John 2:1 NIV My dear children, I write this to you so that you will not sin. But if anybody does sin, we have one who speaks to the Father in our defense-- Jesus Christ, the Righteous One.

The Word was written to us and if we "shama" and "shamar" the Word we will refrain from sin.

We must understand that this does not mean we will never sin. There will be times when we do not yield to the Word; when we do this we give our flesh control and sin will be the result. We have two natures and one will take preeminence based on which one occupies the majority of our time.

When we do sin; however, we have an advocate. Jesus Christ supports us and defends us. He speaks to the Father on our behalf because He has paid the price in full for our sin.

> Romans 4:7-8 NIV "Blessed are they whose transgressions are forgiven, whose sins are covered. Blessed is the man whose sin the Lord will never count against him."

We are so very blessed. Do not fall for the lie that tells us that we cannot go to God when we sin. We have nowhere else to go if we want victory over sin! **Christ is the only answer to our sin problem. When Christ paid the price for your sin He did a complete work and He is there to support you and encourage you; He is not waiting to punish you. This does not mean that God is soft on sin; this means that the punishment for our sin was upon Him and He paid the price for us.**

> Isaiah 53:5 AMP But He was wounded for our transgressions, He was bruised for our guilt and iniquities; the chastisement [needful to obtain] peace and well-being for us was upon Him, and with the stripes [that wounded] Him we are healed and made whole.

Oh! What a Savior! He was punished for me and for you; He paid the price once and for all for all of us. Do not ignore what He did for you and believe that you have to pay a price. Walk in the victory that Christ has obtained for you!

Is your life one of victory or are you controlled by the flesh? We choose everyday whether we are going to yield (or submit) to the Word or to our flesh. When we choose to ignore the Word of God, sin *will* dominate our lives.

> Psalms 119:9 KJV Wherewithal shall a young man cleanse his way? by taking heed [thereto] according to Thy Word.

The phrase "cleanse his way" means to put yourself in a Spiritual position and to travel a Spiritual route. If we are going to walk in the Spirit we are going to have to understand the value of the Word. Sin cannot prevail in the life of a person who abides in the Word. Taking heed was translated from the Hebrew word "shamar." As we noticed previously, this word is also translated as keep and it means to remain focused on, to protect, and to hedge in. We will walk in the Spirit when we hedge the Word about in our lives. Keeping our focus on the Word transports us to a Spiritual position; it keeps us on a Spiritual path. Keeping our focus on the Word brings us into a place of victory over the flesh.

This victory is a gift from God.

1 Corinthians 15:57 NIV But thanks be to God! He gives us the victory through our Lord Jesus Christ.

1 John 5:3 KJV For this is the love of God, that we keep His commandments: and His commandments are not grievous.

The love *of* God, not love *for* God, is the ability to focus on the Word. It is because of His great love for us that He gave us the Word and the ability to "shamar" the Word; as a result of the Word, we experience victory. The Word is not a burden; the Word is our life – it is our life as God has it; it is victory over the sinful nature.

This gift of victory is not something we can boast about; it is something we should be thankful for.

2 Corinthians 3:4-6 NIV Such confidence as this is ours through Christ before God. Not that we are competent in ourselves to claim anything for ourselves, but our competence comes from God. He has made us competent as ministers of a new

covenant--not of the letter but of the Spirit; for the letter kills, but the Spirit gives life.

These verses warrant repeating. **The only confidence we can claim is the confidence that is found in Christ. We are ineffectual on our own; we are useless apart from Christ. If we are going to experience victory over the flesh, we are going to have to remember this.** The truth is found in knowing that we cannot produce Spiritual fruit outside of Christ. Do not grow weary of hearing this.

We are not ministers (attendants) of the law; we are not to attend to rules and regulations. It is *not* our duty to attempt to avoid sin. We are to attend to the Word of God and experience the work that it does in our lives; the Word will give us the victory over sin. The Spirit will give life; the Spirit will produce Spiritual fruit – fruit that is alive and remains. When we attend to the law, we can only expect death.

In living by the law we also find ourselves longing for recognition for what *we* have "accomplished." The law gives honor to man when he can manage to behave accordingly. The law has its focus on man; man is center-stage in this drama of rule upon rule. If man can accomplish what the law dictates then man can pat himself on the back, take a bow, and take a seat. Man can take pride in his works and live a lie.

1 Corinthians 4:7 NIV For who makes you different from anyone else? What do you have that you did not receive? And if you did receive it, why do you boast as though you did not?

The law instigates high-mindedness. It prompts us to desire recognition. Grace reminds us that God deserves the glory.

Be aware of the fact that you are a receiver. Keep your thoughts centered on Christ and what He has provided *for* you, not on what you think you can accomplish on your own. **When we are Spiritually minded we recognize that the Word produced the faith that produced the Spiritual actions.** Spiritual thinking reminds us of the magnitude of the Word.

> Mark 4:24 NIV "Consider carefully what you hear," he continued. "With the measure you use, it will be measured to you--and even more."

God has given each one of us a measure of faith. What are we doing with this measure of faith? Everyone one of us has been given the Word of God. The hearing of the Word produces faith; the Word is our measure of faith. The amount of the Word that is being displayed in our lives depends on what is going on behind closed doors in regards to the Word. Are you desperate for the Word? Are you taking the measure you have been given and using it? The person who is storing the Word up in their life is the person who will receive what the Word has to offer. We cannot expect the Word to come to pass in our lives if we are ignoring it.

What measure are you using? If we are paying little attention, or no attention at all, to the Word and the work it produces in our lives then we are only producing works of the flesh – no matter how "Spiritual" they appear. We are not experiencing victory over our flesh when we are disregarding the Word; instead, we are being dominated by our flesh.

1 John 3:10 MSG Here's how you tell the difference between God's children and the devil's children: The one who won't practice righteous ways isn't from God, nor is the one who won't love brother or sister. A simple test.

This verse is not a test of our salvation. Salvation is based on what Christ did for us – not on our works or what we *think* we are doing for Christ. This verse is a test of our actions. We can realize where we are, in the Spirit or in the flesh, by the fruit we are producing. When we are producing Spiritual fruit it is because we are walking in the nature of Christ; we are living as God's child. Instead of identifying with our flesh, the nature that is of the devil, we are associating with Christ.

In associating with Christ, we will find love active and preeminent. Love is never lacking in the person that associates with who they are in Christ. When we are focusing on our identity in the flesh, it takes us away from love. People who focus on works do not look at love as a priority; in fact, many of them are too angry to love anyone – including themselves. They are in such a state of achievement that they do not have the time to dwell on the love Christ has for them. Love comes full circle, love is displayed to others, only when we are filling ourselves with the love of God that is in Christ Jesus.

We are now Spiritually alive *in Christ*. Where death once exclusively reigned, life has now come in alongside and the rivalry begins. It will be up to us which nature dominates. We can ignore the Spirit and let the flesh reign or we can ignore the flesh and let the Spirit have control. We neglect our flesh by focusing on the Spirit or abiding in the Word of God. The Word of God is our life; it is everything we need to enter into the new nature. The more attention we give to the Word, the less domineering the flesh will be. As we begin to focus more on the new nature (the Word of God) we will find that our flesh is progressively robbed of its power in our lives. This will not be done with ease at all times; the flesh will fight against the Spirit, but we have power in Christ that overcomes all the power of the enemy (Luke 10:19); we have victory over the flesh in Christ.

CHAPTER 15

THE CONCLUSION

Ecclesiastes 12:13 KJV
Let us hear the conclusion of the whole matter:
Fear God, and keep His commandments:
for this [is] the whole [duty] of man.

The conclusion is the end. It is the entirety of the subject being discussed. What was being discussed here in Ecclesiastes was the meaning of life. King Solomon set out to find the significance of life under the sun. He wanted to know what man's purpose was here on earth.

> Ecclesiastes 1:13 KJV And I gave my heart to seek and search out by wisdom concerning all [things] that are done under heaven: this sore travail hath God given to the sons of man to be exercised therewith.

King Solomon wondered why God even placed us here in the first place. Why was man given the burden of living this life under the sun? Why did we have to wake up every day and work and toil only to go to bed and begin again the next day? Life seemed monotonous to King Solomon. It did not appear to be worth living.

> Ecclesiastes 4:1-3 NIV Again I looked and saw all the oppression that was taking place under the sun: I saw the tears of the oppressed-- and they have no

comforter; power was on the side of their oppressors--
and they have no comforter. And I declared that the
dead, who had already died, are happier than the
living, who are still alive. But better than both is he
who has not yet been, who has not seen the evil that is
done under the sun.

As King Solomon kept his focus on this realm alone,
he was disenchanted with all that this life had to offer. He
saw the oppression and the injustice of man and he
determined that man was better off not even being born.

King Solomon had achieved much; nonetheless, he
was not content until he realized the meaning of this life.

King Solomon discovered that the meaning of life
was to fear God and to keep (shamar) His commandments.
We are here on earth to be in awe of God and focus on His
Word and protect His Word in our lives. When we live in
this manner, life will become worth living.

Ecclesiastes 12:13-14 KJV   Let us hear the
conclusion of the whole matter: Fear God, and keep
His commandments: for this [is] the whole [duty] of
man. For God shall bring every work into judgment,
with every secret thing, whether [it be] good, or
whether [it be] evil.

When we are living a life that is focused on the Word
we will produce Spiritual fruit. King Solomon discovered
that we need to revere God and focus on His Word because
one day our actions will be judged. Our actions will be
judged "with every secret thing." What is this "secret thing?"
This phrase comes from a word that means "what is hidden."
Our source, our method of producing fruit, is hidden; no one
can see *how* we do what we do – they can only see *what* we

do. Many actions appear Spiritual, but only the actions that are birthed from the Spirit are, in fact, truly Spiritual.

Since our actions will be seen for what they really are – Spiritual or carnal – it is important for us to fear God and focus on His Word. We must be in awe of God and what He has accomplished in our lives. We must recognize the purpose of His Word; we must see the Word as our very life. We must see the Word as our Spiritual Source. Only the actions that are of the Spirit will be eternal. Any action that we produced outside of Christ will be burned up (1 Corinthians 3:9-15); it will only be a momentary accomplishment.

King Solomon determined that a life lived in the flesh was futile; even still, this life is available to man. We will have to decide if we are going to live this life we are given in the flesh or in the Spirit.

Our two natures will disagree on the purpose of life. The flesh believes that life is all about achievement and self. A life of achievement and self lends itself to weariness, pride, and vanity. This lifestyle of the flesh is focused on man, not on the Lord.

> Ecclesiastes 1:2-3,8 NIV "Meaningless! Meaningless!" says the Teacher. "Utterly meaningless! Everything is meaningless." What does man gain from all his labor at which he toils under the sun? All things are wearisome, more than one can say. The eye never has enough of seeing, nor the ear its fill of hearing.

When life is lived in the flesh, life is meaningless. What we can gain from the flesh is only fleeting; it will not be significant.

Ecclesiastes 2:11 NIV Yet when I surveyed all that my hands had done and what I had toiled to achieve, everything was meaningless, a chasing after the wind; nothing was gained under the sun.

King Solomon realized that his achievements would one day be forgotten and everything he amassed would one day rot away. He did not find any fulfillment in his work.

This lifestyle will wear us out! How hard it is to live a life of trying to perform. Fortunately, **God is not asking us to perform; He is asking us to rely on Him.** When we do anything that is outside of His will for us, we will become frustrated and exhausted. We can never perform well enough to be satisfied. We can never earn enough to feel content. **Only that which is accomplished through Christ will leave us feeling fulfilled.**

We, of necessity, need know the difference between our Spirit and our flesh. We must know how to fight the flesh through the Word of God. As we journey through this life, we must understand what a life lived in the flesh amounts to. We must also understand how amazing a life lived in Christ will be. Take hold of the gift of the new nature you have in Christ and live a life worth living! A life that will continue on into eternity!

More books by Stephanie White:

HEAVEN ON EARTH: it is a life most people believe is not possible to achieve, but according to God's Word that is exactly what we can have! Heaven on Earth takes you on a journey through the Word of God so that you can find out what is available to you as God's child and you will also discover how to enjoy this life to the fullest.

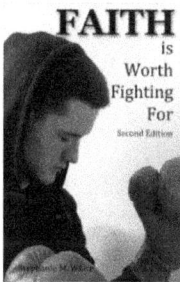

FAITH IS WORTH FIGHTING FOR: In God's Word we discover that we are to live by faith, but we also see that faith is a fight. As a Christian, faith is essential. Eternal value is assigned to our faith. This book is an in-depth study of faith - what faith is, how we obtain it, how it works, what classifies it as genuine, what its benefits are, and more.

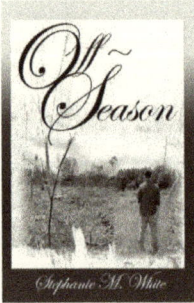

OFF-SEASON Everyone experiences an off-season in life - sometimes more than one. An off-season is a dry time; it is a time of lack and a time of trials. These times can feel daunting and painful; therefore, we must understand the purpose of these times and we must be sure that God has a plan for our good and His glory

A NEW BEGINNING
This devotional is for those who are new to the Word and their walk with God.

https://whitestephanie83.wixsite.com/heavenonearthforyou

www.ingramcontent.com/pod-product-compliance
Lightning Source LLC
Chambersburg PA
CBHW032036040426
42449CB00007B/909